managing talented people

MANAGING TALENTED PEOPLE

getting on with –
and getting the best from –
your top talent

Alan Robertson
& Graham Abbey

www.yourmomentum.com
the stuff that drives you

Manager's momentum – a new suite of management development books for the leaders of the future

We've taken the successful approach of the momentum personal development books – active personal coaching, applied personal values and highly stimulating delivery – and applied it to the portfolio of skills that talented leaders of the future will want and need. The result? A set of books and accelerated learning tools for smart managers that will equip you for a bright future of managing talented people and entrepreneurial ventures.

These are intelligent, inspiring yet practical books on a new breed of essential managerial topics – a far cry from an older style of management book, which too often features the same old tired subjects drowned in dense text, manager's momentum is characterized by edgy, modern subjects delivered in an easily absorbed dynamic style. These are books to make you energized, not tired. And books that you'll be happy to be seen with.

Other manager's momentum titles:
Complete leadership
a practical guide for developing your leadership talents
Susan Bloch and Philip Whiteley

Solution-focused coaching
a manager's guide to getting the best from people
Tony Grant and Jane Greene

Also available – momentum personal development books for the stuff that drives you.
Lead yourself
be where others will follow
Mick Cope

Change activist
make big things happen fast
Carmel McConnell

Innervation
personal training for life and work
Guy Browning

The complete list of momentum personal development titles is available via
www.yourmomentum.com and www.business-minds.com

momentum prescription – Let us help you work out which book will suit your symptoms

*Feel **stuck in a rut**? Something wrong and need help doing something about it?*

◆ If you need tools to help make changes in your life: **coach yourself** (a good general guide to change)

◆ If you are considering dramatic career change: **snap, crackle or stop**

◆ If you need to work out what you'd like to be doing and how to get there: **be your own career consultant**

◆ If you need help making things happen and tackling the 'system' at work/in life: **change activist**

◆ If you think you want more from your life than a 'normal' career: **careers un-ltd**

*Feel that you **can never make decisions** and you just let things 'happen'?*

◆ If you need help making choices: **the big difference**

◆ If you want to feel empowered and start making things happen for yourself: **change activist**

*Feel life is **too complicated and overwhelming**?*

◆ If you need help working through office politics and complexity: **clued up**

◆ If you need a kick up the backside to get out of your commerce-induced coma: **change activist**

◆ If you need an amusing and very helpful modern life survival guide: **innervation**

◆ If you never have enough time or energy to get things done or think properly: **mental space**

*Feel like you might be in the **wrong job**?*

◆ If you want help finding your destiny job and inspiration to make that dramatic career change: **snap, crackle or stop**

◆ If you feel like you aren't doing a job that is really 'what you are about': **soultrader**

◆ If you want to feel empowered and start making things happen for yourself: **change activist**

◆ If you think you want more from your life than a 'normal' career: **careers un-ltd**

Feel that you're not the person/leader you should be?

◆ If you want to be the kind of person others want to follow: **lead yourself**

◆ If you feel your working relationships with people could improve: **managing yourself**

◆ If you need help becoming the person you've always wanted to be: **reinvent yourself**

◆ If you want to work out everything you've got to offer, and how to improve that: **grow your personal capital**

Feel you need help getting your ideas into action?

◆ If the problem is mainly other people, lack of time and the messiness of life: **clued up**

◆ If the problem is communicating your thinking: **hey you!**

◆ If the problem is getting things across to other people: **managing yourself**

◆ If the problem is more ideas than time and you are a bit overwhelmed by work: **mental space**

◆ If the problem is making change in your life: **coach yourself**

Feel you aren't projecting yourself and managing your career as well as you should?

◆ If you'd like to be the kind of person people think of first: **managing brand me**

◆ If you'd like people to listen to your ideas more readily: **hey you!**

◆ If you'd like to come across as the person you really are inside: **soultrader**

◆ If you need general help in changing the way you work/live: **coach yourself**

◆ If you need help working out what you've got and how best to use it: **float you**

Feel you'd like to be much more creative and a real 'ideas person'

◆ If you need inspiration on how to be innovative and think creatively: **innervation**

◆ If you need help spreading your ideas and engendering support: **hey you!**

PEARSON EDUCATION LIMITED

Edinburgh Gate
Harlow CM20 2JE
Tel: +44 (0)1279 623623
Fax: +44 (0)1279 431059
www.pearsoned.co.uk

First published in Great Britain in 2003

© Pearson Education Limited 2003

The right of Alan Robertson and Graham Abbey to be identified as authors of this work has been asserted by them in accordance with the Copyright, Designs and Patents Act 1988.

ISBN 1843 04024 7

British Library Cataloguing in Publication Data
A CIP catalogue record for this book can be obtained from the British Library.

10 9 8 7 6 5 4 3 2

Typeset by Northern Phototypesetting Co. Ltd, Bolton
Printed and bound in Great Britain by Henry Ling Ltd, Dorchester

The Publishers' policy is to use paper manufactured from sustainable forests.

our thanks to...

Melanie Armstrong, Sally Atkinson, David Bolchover, Maxine Bradley, David and Jane Dorman, Justine Drew, Brenda Eisenberg, Kevin Eyre, Paul Gaskin, Claire Holloway, Kate Jenkins, Michelle Kearsey, Jack Lang, Dana Lawrence, Tuhi Leef, Malcolm and Ruth Levene, Sinead McBrearty, Carol Moran, Marian O'Brien, Sarah Pegman, Nancy Prendergast, Andrew Ross, Grace Sim, Richard Stagg, Rachael Stock, Nicki Tanner, Rakhi Taylor and Friends, Mike Usher-Clark, Jonathan Winter.

Love and special thanks as always to Kate and to Hilary, Caitlin, Mark and Katie.

introduction

Puzzling in a danger zone

Here's a puzzle.

If organizations are so aware of the need to retain talent, then why do they not seem to be getting better at doing it?

It was a report by management consultants McKinsey in 1996 that first explored and articulated the War for Talent, yet when it was updated late in 2000 it indicated that the issue was becoming more rather than less urgent.

Here's another puzzle, which may have something to do with the first.

Why are the most talented often the most rewarding people to have in your team and yet, at the same time, the most challenging to manage?

In the frenzy of publications spawned by the 'Talent Wars' this question, the one likely to be of the greatest relevance and use to individual managers, remains curiously neglected. Most of the advice has been focused at an organizational level on issues such as 'how to become a company that talent wants to work for' or 'recruiting and retaining talent'.

And here's a third. (You'll have gathered that we like puzzles. They point to where there is an opportunity to make a difference.)

What exactly do people mean by talent anyway?

It is our belief that answering the third question is the key to unlocking the other puzzles. There is a fundamental lack of clarity about what is meant by talented. This creates confusion and misunderstanding, because it obscures underlying differences in expectation. And it is the tensions between these different expectations that makes managing talented people so challenging.

This book explores those expectations, clarifies the underlying tensions and provides a practical approach for managing them.

A summary of the plot

Of course, businesses need talented people. Any domain, which is complex and competitive, dynamic and innovative, is obviously going to need talented people. You don't need yet another book to tell you that. We're taking that proposition for granted.

We also take it as read that the need for talent is now more acute than ever before. The demand for talented people reflects a fundamental structural shift in the nature of work, whatever temporary economic downturns might lead you to believe. If you aren't convinced about that, or you haven't thought much about it, then you might like to look at the argument. We've summarized it at the back of the book, as a 'prequel', for your reference, if you need it.

This book is not another exhortation to recognize that the talent issue is urgent. It is an invitation to consider why it remains unresolved and to explore what can be done about that, at the practical level of day-to-day management. Our starting point is this . . .

Talented people are not easy to manage.

Why is that? And what can you do about it?

What exactly is the difficulty? Part of the problem is that what 'talent' signifies remains stubbornly unclear. This may seem bizarre for such a well-publicized concern. But, as we will show, talent remains a fuzzy concept. And while this is convenient in some respects, at least in the short term and especially perhaps for managers, that convenience comes with a significant price ticket attached – because talent is not unilaterally defined by management.

What 'talent' signifies remains stubbornly unclear.

Talent is a set of expectations. A complex set. Some of these expectations are managerial. Some are those of the talented. But many are unclear. And from that lack of clarity come most of the difficulties of managing talented people. The problems of great, but mixed, expectations.

What are we going to do to help?

◆ We will provide help to deal with talented people.

◆ We will clarify the various expectations that are bundled up in the concept of talent. We're going to disentangle the idea and make sense of it. We're going to provide a working definition, by which we mean a definition that will work, one that you can use in practice. Because our interest is in the practical.

◆ We will look at the broader implications for your role as a manager. Because managing talented people requires a distinctive type of leadership.

◆ We are going to illustrate the sorts of challenges that occur when it comes to managing talented people, uncover what is going on below the surface, and explain the approaches that you can take in order to handle these challenges more successfully.

◆ We will provide a framework to allow you to plan your approach to your talented people, helping you resolve any problems you may anticipate.

A word of caution: you can't 'manage' talented people in the conventional sense of the word. If you're looking for some new and subtle means of control, then you are in for a disappointment – because talented people are essentially uncontrollable.

Success in managing talented people is founded in a different type of relationship and in a different quality of dialogue. It requires the manager of talented people to take a distinct and additive role to what the talented people can do for themselves.

And, given the nature of talented people, it is a role which is only temporary.

Since time is of the essence, that is probably enough by way of an introduction. Let us give you a few comments on how the book is arranged and then you can get on with it.

Making this book work for you

To be practical, this book must support you becoming skilful in dealing with your actual difficulties in managing talented people. That's tricky for two reasons. Your 'actual difficulties' will not be the same as the next person's. And different people learn in different ways.

A widely accepted picture of the learning process recognizes it as a continuing cycle with four distinct elements, each of which can be used as an individual's preferred starting point.

We have therefore arranged this book in four parts, each corresponding to one of these approaches to learning. *Reflecting on talented people* uses multiple perspectives to consider the definition of talent. *A theory on managing talented people* makes a sense of these different perspectives and presents our set of principles for managing talent. For those who find theories too distant from what they have to actually do, *The practice of managing talented people* looks at just that – what you actually have to do. The final part, *Managing talent in action*, is short, because actively doing it lies outside any book. That domain is yours. We provide a framework to assist you to work through your own situation, a companion for your activity.

TAKING PART
ACTIVELY

MAKING USE OF
EXPERIENCE

REFLECTING ON
EXPERIENCE

MAKING SENSE
OF EXPERIENCE

There is no 'right' sequence to these four parts. We'd rather you called them John, Paul, George and Ringo (four icons of talent) than thought of them as Parts 1, 2, 3 and 4.

For those of you short of time (that'll be all of you then), each part has been written to stand alone. Dip in and out as you see fit. Take away whatever you find useful.

reflecting on talented people

a theory on managing talented people

the practice of managing talented people

3 – Delivering skilfully / 160

managing talent in action

A plan of action / 182

reflecting on talented people

This part of the book considers a number of different angles on what is understood by – and consequently expected of – talent. The absence of a shared understanding of these expectations makes it inherently difficult to manage talented people. We explore where these different understandings come from and some of the implications of holding them. (Because it's an exploration this section may at times feel slower and more disjointed than other parts of the book.)

You are likely to find this bit particularly valuable if you want a deeper understanding of why managing talented people is, by its nature, a challenging activity and if you want to invest the time to assimilate and appreciate the perspectives of the different stakeholders.

who defines talent?

If we're going to be good at managing talented people, then we'd better be clear about who they are. What is talent? What do we mean by talented people? Who says so? And what exactly are they saying?

Turns out that these are difficult questions, more challenging than you might expect for a phenomenon that has received so much publicity in recent years.

That's the core theme running through this first part of the book. What do people mean by talent?

The core learning style here is reflecting on the experiences of those involved. This makes for a chapter rich in insight, with many views represented. We do summarize and synthesize these views as we go, but our main aim is to get you thinking (and reflecting).

Our main aim is to get you thinking (and reflecting).

Before we get started let's listen to one manager, Anne-Marie, talk about talent. Listen for the issues, the contradictions, the threads of ideas, all of which we will return to. Anne-Marie is an American in her early 40s who has been working in the UK for the past 10 years, building her career in strategic marketing communications.

As managers we simply don't think enough about how to manage talented people. But how do we make space to do it?

Those I have worked with are often not aware of their talent – we tend to discover it together. On the one hand, people with talent stand out, if only because of their impact, their performance, yet it is not obvious exactly how to define talent. It is certainly something to do with the ability to get at the root of the issue, to synthesize information and come up with a solution. In part it is discipline, to think, to get a feeling for the situation and to drive it forward – if you can't apply it, then it's not talent. But it is also about having a broader perspective, an intellectual curiosity.

The talented seem restless, though perhaps that is simply a feature of the young. Consequently, they need a lot of encouragement and nurture. They virtually demand constant positive feedback and help in seeing where what they are doing is taking them. They are not always good at looking into the future. When first presented with a problem, especially if it is abstract, they need guidance, to get going. Once they are, I am still amazed at how often they come up with things that blow me away.

It is not entirely comfortable to be a manager of talent. I still have the sense that as the manager I should know everything. Talent has a way of making you feel inadequate or intimidated. They expect the usual stuff from you, respect, opportunity, guidance, but also want to be left alone. That can be tricky – finding the right level. You have the faith they will do well, you don't need close contact, but at the same time have to know when to intervene.

Social skills are important. They act as a lubricant, soften some of the rougher edges. Talent is linked with creativity and this ability has to be supported by 'good skills' in order to produce outstanding performance. Teaching good skills is an important role for managers, but it is almost too big, it takes up too much time.

Boy, we need to give this more thought.

With the talent wars raging, you would expect someone to have done the thinking to which Anne-Marie refers – to be clear by now on a

reflecting on talented people

managing talented people

momentum

definition of talent. But it seems that people still tend to be either fuzzy or narrow in their understanding of 'talent'.

What happened when we asked people?

Everybody thinks they're talented

Everybody thinks they're talented. Don't they? Try asking people. 'Are you talented?' Hear what they say.

'I have some talents.'

'In some respects.'

'It depends on what. I have certain talents.'

What do you expect them to say? *'Yes. Of course.'* They tend not to say that. Too cocky. Too self-assured. Too much risk of inviting a put down, if not now, then at some time in the future. If they do say it, then they give the words a strong inoculation of humour, so that they have an escape route if they are challenged.

So what can they say? *'Me, talented? No. Certainly not.'* They can't say that either, can they? Too self-effacing. Too much risk of undermining their prospects, destroying their chances when it comes to the next pay review or the next promotion panel. Too much danger of giving an unscrupulous manager an easy target when it comes to making difficult choices like how to allocate the bonus pool or how to ensure that at least some of the performance ratings are categorized 'below average'.

Risky places, organizations. Making *'Are you talented?'* a tricky question. We've asked that question many times in the course of researching this book, and we've watched people closely as they've answered. And the responses have all been careful, slightly guarded, variations on the same theme. *'In some ways'*, they say. Here's our favourite.

'Are you talented?'

'Hmm . . . That's a loaded question . . . I'd like to think so.'

That's a loaded question. Someone put it into words. The talent question is political. It involves people's interests. The personal stakes are high. And organizations, gatherings of people, places where interests inevitably compete are therefore places where it is not easy to speak openly about talent.

The talent question is political. It involves people's interests. The personal stakes are high.

But the people who work for you do care about the definition of talent. It's always going to matter to them.

'Are my talents recognized?'

'Are my talents being developed?'

'Are my talents being wasted?'

Questions that talented people ask themselves.

'How talented are you?'

'Are you one of our key people?'

'Are we making best use of your talents?'

Questions that managers need to be asking.

Important questions. But questions that are seldom in the open. Questions that are seldom the subject of frank and open dialogue. Answers that may exist are imprecise and fuzzy. This enables managers and talented people to appear to share views on talent, but at the same time hedge their bets. Precision leaves no room for manoeuvre, no room to flex your position depending on the audience.

The political nature of talent is a significant cause of the fuzzy definitions of talent in operation. Furthermore, the definition of talent becomes skewed. It is management that gets to define 'talented'.

So before returning to how the talented describe themselves, what do managers say and believe about talent?

the managerial definition of talent

Perhaps you think it doesn't matter that most people find it difficult to talk openly about whether they are talented. Perhaps it's more convenient that way; there is certainly less potential for embarrassment. After all, you might say, surely it is a question for the managers to answer. Who is talented? Who has the most to offer? Who is of the greatest value for the organization? Who deserves to progress?

You might want to pause and think about these questions in relation to your own people for a moment.

Or you might choose just to read on.

What is certain is that these are questions that, sooner or later, you will need to address as a manager. They are part and parcel of your responsibility. A greater part, a bigger parcel than ever before. So how do managers go about answering the question? Let's start with a provocative generalization. It is a generalization, but it's derived from our experience.

How do managers tend to define talent? Quickly. Personally. Imprecisely. That's how.

What do we mean? Here's a set of questions we use in organizations which regularly reveals these tendencies. Try the questions out for yourself. Get a group of managers together and ask them. You have to ask the questions in sequence. Get the answer to the first before you ask the next, and so on.

Question 1: who are the talented people in your department?

Managers generally come up with ready answers to this question. They will name the name, or, more usually give you a list. Because, after all, this is a political question for them too. Too few people identified as talented in their department and it won't reflect well on them. Too many and there's a danger that they'll be called upon to share their talented people with some other department. Hmm . . . tricky. But they almost invariably produce some names, and they do this quickly.

So far, so good.

Question 2: what exactly makes these people talented?

Eh? Pardon? Could you repeat the question? In our experience managers seldom produce ready answers to this question. They find it harder. They find it easier to tell you who the talented people are, but much more difficult to explain what it is about these people that makes them talented. Anne-Marie hinted at the same.

Is it because this is another politically 'loaded' question? It would appear not. It seems to be rather that they simply haven't thought about the question. When you do probe, and help them to think about it, then you tend to uncover a variety of answers and we will look at those shortly. For the moment, the point is that managers tend to identify talent 'personally'. And we mean personally both in the sense that they have their own, generally unconscious, definition of talent and also in the sense that they recognize the talented person rather than the ingredients of talent.

OK, so what's the third question?

Question 3: what are you doing to develop that talent?

We don't usually even get asked to repeat this question. More commonly there is an embarrassed silence and an avoidance of eye contact, until finally someone suggests a course that they're planning to send one of their people on. Awkward. But of course, it's going to be difficult to develop talent if you're not clear what it is. If you're fuzzy about it. Imprecise.

Quickly. Personally. Imprecisely. In our experience this is how managers tend to answer questions about who is talented. And these are pointers to 'default thinking' on the subject, clues that most managers do not give enough good thinking to the question. We will return to good thinking in the third part of this book. There we look at what capability you need to manage talented people well. For now good thinking is the higher-quality thinking that is required for issues where the stakes are high. (As they are when it comes to managing talented people. The stakes are very high in the talent wars.)

Default thinking is 'hasty, narrow, fuzzy and sprawling'. Or quick, personal, imprecise. Good thinking, by contrast, means giving time to thinking, organizing it, opening it up to more possibilities, and deepening your understanding of what's going on, how things work and how to make things happen.

So, before we go deeper, how were your own answers to the three questions? Quick? Personal? Imprecise?

Perhaps our generalization is too harsh in your own case. (We said it was going to be provocative.) After all, you must be someone who is interested in managing talented people to have picked this book up in the first place. But we hope you find the provocation useful rather than offensive. It's a way of calling attention to the need for managers to be clearer about what they mean by talented.

We've already made the point that the definition of what is meant by talent is effectively treated as management's prerogative. We've now indicated that management as a rule finds it difficult to articulate what it means by talent.

Danger signals, don't you think?

Talent as superior performance

We've established that managers generally find it easier to say who is talented than to explain what they mean by that. What does that tell us?

It suggests that the commonest way to define talent is by reference to the individual's performance. Ask managers why someone appears on their talent list and they'll tell you it's because that person is a good performer.

And this is an entirely reasonable definition. Talent is superior performance. It makes complete sense, at least from a management perspective. That's what you want, after all. Superior performers.

So managers, not anonymous organizations, tend to define talent in terms of outcomes, delivering the goods, getting the job done better than others. What does 'better' mean? More quickly, more reliably, more effectively. Again, the explanation rapidly becomes fuzzy and imprecise. What is clear, or at least easy to grasp, is that talent is about superior performance, about results. That's why talent tends to be defined personally and imprecisely. It's easier to see who delivers superior results, much harder to get behind that and explain how they do it.

Talent is about superior performance, about results. That's why talent tends to be defined personally and imprecisely. It's easier to see who delivers superior results, much harder to get behind that and explain how they do it.

Which leaves talent rather like that old comment about art. *'I can't exactly tell you what I like, but I know it when I see it.'*

Difficult to see how you set about managing talented people in that case. That's the trouble with defining talent in terms of performance. It's easy to see it, much less easy to see how you get it, or keep it.

Talent as 'the right stuff'

On the other hand, you can define talent in terms of characteristics. You can define it in terms of ingredients.

This is the approach that lies behind the great interest that some managers have taken in 'competencies' and competency frameworks over recent years since the original work by Richard Boyatzis (*The Competent Manager*, Wiley, 1982). A competency is essentially an underlying characteristic that produces superior performance. Many companies – yours is probably one of them – now have more or less elaborate lists of these desirable characteristics: *managing group process, conceptual flexibility, customer focus, proactive orientation, stamina and adaptability* . . . and so on. The lists are long and various.

And that's another problem. There's no agreed list of the necessary ingredients. There is, on the other hand, no shortage of opinions. Consider some recent examples.

The first comes from an advertisement in the appointments pages calling for 'Young Retail High Fliers'. It sought to attract *'the world's very best commercial talent – prickly, focused, intolerant and shrewd achievers who share a determination to maximize their career and achieve substantive personal wealth.'*

So, are *'prickly, focused, intolerant and shrewd'* (always supposing that we could recognize these things when we saw them) the magic ingredients?

A very different looking list appears in the book *High Flyers – Developing the Next Generation of Leaders* (Harvard Business School Press, 1998) by former director of research at the Center for Creative Leadership, Morgan W. McCall, Jr, where the characteristics of future global executives are identified as follows. They:

◆ seek opportunities to learn;

◆ act with integrity;

◆ adapt to cultural differences;

◆ are committed to making a difference;

- seek broad business knowledge;
- bring out the best in people;
- are insightful: see things from new angles;
- have the courage to take risks;
- seek and use feedback;
- learn from mistakes;
- are open to criticism.

Here's a third view. This one comes from our own research. It's the opinion of a FTSE-100 human resource director, expressed in interview.

What are the essential ingredients of 'talent'?

'Difficult question! It depends so much on the situation. Probably some adaptiveness, open-mindedness, some degree of resilience, some ongoing curiosity, the ever-present need to keep learning; they will tend to have good self-awareness and agency. They're people who will find something to do, will seek feedback and find ways of getting it. Real talent seems to work in tandem with the enterprise. It's not just individualistic, there's some intelligent adaptation.'

Three different opinions. The first capturing the beliefs of a self-made millionaire entrepreneur, seeking to recruit in his own self-image. Reflecting a particular set of experiences in a particular domain, emphasizing commercial achievement. The second embodying the findings of a business school researcher's extensive investigations across different business sectors, emphasizing personal learning. The third being the spontaneous, but clearly thoughtful, response of a practising human resource professional. Similar to the second, but with an explicit accent on the need for adaptation to the organization's agenda.

All three vary. Yet all three point to the common factor in all managerial definitions of talent.

Different ways of looking at the same thing

Whether one goes about it by spotting the people, or by spotting the ingredients, essentially, these two approaches to defining talent are simply different ways of looking at the same thing, which is performance. The first way – who is talented? – makes an overall, holistic, intuitive assessment. The second way – what is talent and therefore who is talented? – takes a bottom-up, analytical, objective approach. Either way, the aim is to make a judgement about performance, often the expectation of future high performance. The first way is easier, certainly quicker and understandably widely used in practice. The second way is more complex, widely advocated by human resource professionals, can have much to offer but is, understandably, more time-consuming and demanding for time-pressed managers to adopt in practice.

Our purpose here is not to argue the merits of one approach over the other. Plenty of inky gunpowder and paper shot has been expended on that subject elsewhere. Making an intuitive judgement about someone that you can't then explain in more detail seems to us to be obviously risky, just as analysis seems like a poor use of time and effort unless it is purposeful and to the point. And anyway the two approaches are not mutually exclusive. The smart strategy is to achieve a thoughtful and useful balance between the two, as your situation requires. In that sense managing talented people is simply yet another managerial responsibility that calls for active thinking and thoughtful action. The point we want to bring to your attention is about the underlying similarity of the two approaches.

They both define talent in terms of performance. That much is fairly obvious. They both involve judgements. One is more subjective, the other is more objective, but they both involve judgements in the last resort. Less obvious, and more significant in accounting for the practical difficulties that managers experience when it comes to managing talented people, is that both ways of defining talent are actually about expectations.

In short, the definition of talent used in practice by managers appears to be that:

Talented people are expected, by their managers, to produce superior performance both now and in the future.

A matter of expectations

Expectations. This is the unobvious dimension that lies at the heart of all definitions of talent. A time dimension that stretches into the future.

Who is talented? looks at the individual's performance, past and present, and extrapolates a judgement, an assumption perhaps, but an evaluation nevertheless, that a similar quality of performance can also be expected in the future.

What is talent? looks for the rocket fuel that is believed, wrongly or rightly, to propel effective performance, gauges people to see whether they have this on board and then it too makes a judgement about the quality of performance that can be expected in the future.

So managerial definitions of talent are about expectations. Let's not go more deeply for the moment into the quality of these expectations. They may be hopes, aspirations or delusions. They may be more or less realistic, more or less well-founded, but they are always futuristic. When managers apply the label 'talented' to someone, they are branding that person with expectations. Managers may not, in practice generally do not, express these expectations very clearly.

But 'talent' is about expectations.

Hold on! Is performance really the only expectation managers have about talent? It may be the dominant explicit explanation, but is there something hidden, something implied in how managers act towards talented people? Something below the surface?

an underlying expectation

We are arguing that talent is a set of expectations. And that the challenge at the heart of managing talented people is that these expectations are not sufficiently well understood. Part of the difficulty is that not enough attention is given to the expectations that talented people bring to the employment relationship, which we will explore a little later. But another part of the problem is that managers do not think carefully enough about what they want from talent.

As one of our managerial interviewees put it, *'You know, as we talk about this, what strikes me is that we managers don't think enough about this.'*

But can we discern any particular expectations? Although, as we have seen, managerial definitions of talent can incorporate a whole range of different ingredients, with the result that any agreed definition remains underdeveloped, fuzzy and prone to misunderstanding, is there any shape in the fog? We believe there is.

It's hard for people to turn the pattern into words. Ask them. They'll say: *'So and so is clearly talented. You know. It's obvious. They're really good at what they do. They're a cut above the rest.'*

Once again, these are comments about performance. They underline something we mentioned earlier, that people seem to find it easier to identify who is talented than to explain what makes that person talented.

So, if that's the easiest way to do it, let's work with that. Forget the search for ingredients for a moment. Set aside the attempt to articulate specific expectations. Let's work with intuition. Who do you think is talented? We're not asking you to think, this time, about people who work for you or who are known to you personally. In this case, we're asking you to think about the question more generally.

What sorts of people are talented?

This may seem like an odd question, or a tautology, but bear with us. It seems to us that the epithet 'talented' is not equally distributed. It appears to be applied to some occupations much more often than it is to others. We could give you some examples, and we will, but first, we'd like to invite you to think about this question for yourself.

In what sorts of jobs, roles, occupations does the label 'talented' *often* seem to be used? Come up with a few examples that occur to you.

In what sorts of jobs, roles, occupations does the label 'talented' *seldom* seem to be used? Again, come up with your own examples.

So, what did you come up with? And can you see any pattern emerging?

We conducted a little survey around these questions. It wasn't a piece of heavy-duty research, and it wasn't intended to be. We were looking for clues, looking to see if there were any patterns in how people apply the label 'talented'. Because if there were a pattern, then that would give us a lead, which we could pursue to obtain a deeper insight into people's expectations of talent.

We've had inputs from about 30 people, working in various jobs and organizations. As the results came in, a pattern began to emerge almost at once, and as further results came in they simply added to the evidence.

What did we find? The results are intriguing.

We asked for up to five nominations in each category. Here are the top five from our survey, the jobs that were identified most frequently.

Occupations where the label 'talented' is *often* used:

1   artist

2   actor/actress

3   musician

4   sportsperson

5   writer.

Occupations where the label 'talented' is *seldom* used:

1   driving and delivery jobs

2   clerical and administrative jobs

3   builders and assemblers

4   managers

5   accountants and bankers.

Hmm . . .

Interesting, and a bit alarming, to see where managers come in the list, especially as many of our respondents were managers themselves. Managers were mentioned as 'seldom labelled talented' even more frequently than cleaners and labourers.

So what's the pattern? What do you see here? Is it simply that one list consists of the sort of jobs that achieve celebrity, and perhaps wealth, whereas the other is a list of more anonymous, less well-paid occupations? That doesn't quite seem to fit. There are certainly some managers, bankers and accountants who are pretty well paid. And there are plenty of artists, musicians and sportspeople who are not.

There's something else going on in these lists. It's something to do with freedom of expression and creativity.

An expectation of creativity

Labelling someone 'talented' revolves around an expectation of creativity.

Let's explain this expectation by saying some more about what emerged from our survey results. The top five occupations, although they were the dominant groups by a large margin in each case, were only part of the story. There were several other features which we believe to be significant.

The number of different occupations put forward for the 'often labelled talented' list was only half the size of the 'seldom labelled talented', 22 against 43. So 'talented' seems to be the exception rather than the rule. Now in one respect, that's no surprise. 'Talented' always tends to carry a sense of exceptional. But remember that the survey is looking at occupations, not individuals. Do the results mean that there are fewer jobs in which it is possible to be talented? Or to be readily perceived as talented by others? Perhaps that the two categories of jobs differ in some fundamental way?

'Talented' always tends to carry a sense of exceptional.

The idea of some basic difference was supported by the fact that there was very little overlap between the two lists. Jobs tended to feature either on one or the other. The only roles which occurred on both sides of the divide were teachers, managers, doctors and chefs. Oh, and journalists, who tended to figure on the 'often talented' list but made one appearance on the 'seldom' list.

Doctors, along with dentists and health workers, appeared regularly as 'seldom labelled talented'. The only medical people who featured as 'often talented' were surgeons and ground-breaking medical researchers.

The 'talented' label doesn't seem to be to do with 'worth', although the fact that politicians, civil servants and 'white van man' appeared on the 'seldom' list might tempt us to believe that this was a factor in people's thinking. In fact, our respondents often added comments to their replies to indicate that jobs which they were listing as 'seldom labelled talented' were ones which, in their view, made an invaluable contribution to society. Healthcare workers, firemen and lifeboatmen, were all examples.

Remember that our question was not, who is talented and who is not? The question is about which jobs tend to be labelled talented and which do not.

The overall message from the two lists is that creative jobs tend to attract the label talented. Other types of jobs, although they can be highly diverse in terms of the level of skill and training involved, ranging from night watchman to airline pilot, do not.

So creativity seems to be a central ingredient in our expectations of talent.

We tested this out by analysing both lists in terms of an established classification of occupations. John Holland is an American psychologist, and long recognized as a leading international authority on vocational patterns. Through extensive researches into people and occupational environments, Holland has developed a model of distinct personality types. This is a classification, which describes and explains individual differences and has been used to assist in explaining career choices, job attraction and satisfaction, role compatibility and retention: important issues for those who have to manage talented people.

In essence, Holland's model distinguishes six personality types, the Realistic, the Investigative, the Social, the Enterprising, the Conventional and the Artistic.

The definitions of these types are shown below.

The **Realistic** type prefers to work with the tangible, with machines, tools and things. These people see themselves as pragmatic and reliable, with essentially mechanical rather than social skills. They value material rewards for solid achievements. Other people tend to see them as normal, uncomplicated and frank.

The **Investigative** type prefers work which may well involve observable phenomena, but which is more abstract, more conceptual. They see themselves as analytical and intelligent and like to use their critical faculties to explore and explain. They value the acquisition and development of knowledge and understanding. Others often see them as intellectual and not particularly social.

The **Social** type wants work which involves helping and supporting others. They see themselves as caring, empathic and interpersonally skilful. They value concern for the well-being of others. They generally come across to other people as patient, agreeable and helpful.

The **Enterprising** type enjoys work that involves selling ideas and influencing others. They see themselves as confident, purposeful and powerful and they value material accomplishment and social status. Others can find them energetic and persuasive, but also dominant and manipulative.

The **Conventional** type prefers work which revolves around the establishment and maintenance of routines, procedures and standards. They see themselves as organized and disciplined, as stewards and custodians. They value predictability, specifications, order and dependability. Others find them careful and conformist.

The **Artistic** type looks for a working environment that will allow for imagination, originality and creativity. They see themselves as innovative, independent-minded, unconventional and open to experience. They value self-expression of ideas and feelings. Others see the creativity but at the same time often perceive them as disorderly and non-conformist.

We cross-checked all the jobs that were mentioned in our survey with Holland's categorization of those occupations. It revealed a very clear underlying pattern. First, look at the distribution of the jobs that appeared in the 'often labelled talented' list.

More than two-thirds of the jobs that were identified as 'often labelled talented' fall in the Artistic category. None of the other categories comes anywhere close to this. And, also significantly, absolutely none of these 'often labelled talented' jobs belonged in the Conventional category, which, in Holland's view, is the most diametrically different type to the Artistic.

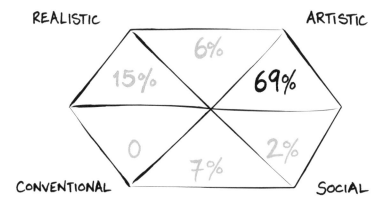

INVESTIGATIVE

REALISTIC

6%

15%

69%

0

7%

2%

CONVENTIONAL

SOCIAL

ENTERPRISING

Look now at the distribution of the jobs that appeared in our 'seldom labelled talented' list.

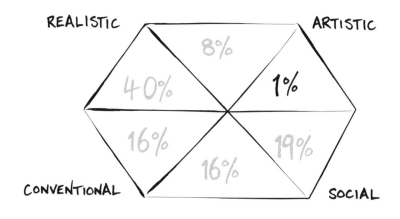

INVESTIGATIVE

REALISTIC

ARTISTIC

8%

40%

1%

16%

16%

19%

CONVENTIONAL

SOCIAL

ENTERPRISING

See the connection with the previous diagram? Artistic types tend not to appear on the 'seldom labelled talented' list. At 1% (that stray journalist we mentioned earlier), it's almost unheard of. So this reinforces the previous finding. But notice that it is not simply the Conventional types who are seldom labelled talented. That fate befalls virtually all the other types in pretty equal measure. If one particular type emerges as least likely to be labelled talented, then it is the Realistics. These are jobs like drivers, builders, mechanics, technicians.

But here's an interesting point. The Realistic type is also the second most likely to feature in the 'often labelled talented' list, although a long way behind the Artistic types. The 'often talented' Realistic types were the sportspersons, plus a handful of chefs and a gardener, these latter probably reflecting current fashions in television celebrity.

So, most people in Realistic jobs are unlikely to be regarded as talented. But a few are. It looks as if level of performance is the differentiator. As Holland points out, the Realistic work environment demands and rewards practical accomplishment and tangible results. It's not surprising then that our survey separated the Realistic types into the high performers and the rest. After all, we have already seen that this is how the managerial world tends to define talented people, in terms of those who deliver manifestly superior performance.

But what are we to make of the way in which the Artistic type dominates our lists? What might this signify?

What it suggests to us is that the biggest single element in our expectations of talented people is that they should be creative. So the expectation on talent is not simply that it should be a superior performer; it must also demonstrate ingenuity and originality. We expect talented people not simply to achieve high standards, but to create new standards, to be innovative, to take things onward and upward.

We expect this. But do we say so? Do we make this expectation clear? Given the difficulty that so many people, not just managers, have in explaining what they mean by talent, it is hardly surprising to find that this expectation of creativity is not always spelled out. Not surprising to find that talent is lost to organizations because of a failure to let it know that it was okay to be ingenious and innovative.

But perhaps that sounds like nonsense. Surely all organizations are unequivocal in calling for innovation and in encouraging creativity? Surely this is what underpins the demand for continuous improvement? In theory, yes. But in practice, do managers consistently welcome that creativity? Do their actions support the organizational rhetoric?

Do yours? When one of your talented people comes to you with a creative idea, what do you do? We're not suggesting that you should mindlessly embrace every whim. Idea-generators can, after all, be notoriously poor when it comes to screening the quality and realism of their brainchildren. But do you consistently give their creativity a hearing? Do you give time to exploring the ideas. Do you allow freedom of expression?

And even if you think you do, is this how you come across to your talented people? There's often a gap here. A gap between our intentions and our impact. We mean to sound encouraging. We mean to make time. But we're under pressure too. We don't have enough time for our own scheduled tasks and priorities. We get tired and impatient.

So when was the last time you failed to make time for a talented person? Failed to listen to an idea that they wanted to pursue? Or failed to listen carefully enough for them to feel they had been given a fair hearing? Because this is the point.

So when was the last time you failed to make time for a talented person?

It would be nice to think that we didn't have to. It would be convenient to believe that talented people will simply be self-starters and get on with things. Easy to say that if they are genuinely talented, then they won't wait to be allowed, won't need to consult us first.

But get real. Organizations aren't like that and we know it. There are always rules, procedures and obligations, approvals that need to be obtained, authorities that need to be satisfied. However talented you are, you can't just ignore these and expect to survive and prosper in the organizational context. As a manager of up-and-coming talent, you are in the middle of that minefield.

This is a central tension for talented people in organizations.

They are expected to be ingenious and innovative. They like to be ingenious and innovative. But that can easily come across as rebellious and non-conformist. Because they are. They can be high impact, but also high maintenance. A mixed blessing.

Think again about the talented people you have known. Here's a little organizer. Where would you place each of them on this map?

HIGH IMPACT, LOW MAINTENANCE	HIGH IMPACT, HIGH MAINTENANCE
LOW IMPACT, LOW MAINTENANCE	LOW IMPACT, HIGH MAINTENANCE

Now, be candid. How did you feel about them? How did you refer to each of them? What was it about the way they behaved that prompted you to put them in each category?

We're facing another aspect of Holland's findings about the Artistic type. They like to see themselves as independent-minded. And organizations are ambivalent, to say the least, about encouraging that. Because these people can be hard work.

Yes, we know it's tempting to come up with that old riposte, 'If you think the talented are hard work, you should try working with the untalented!' But people who are low impact and low maintenance are a much simpler proposition. We have no reason to put up with that. And we trust that you don't. It is the high impact, high maintenance folk who make us feel most ambivalent, who are most demanding on us as managers.

So the question becomes, how do we respond to the challenge of managing talented people, when they demand high maintenance? The idealistic answer is straightforward. We invest in their development. We nurture and coach them. Yes, sure. We all know the principles. But is this what happens in practice in your organization? Is that what you do? Are you an exemplar?

Because in practice managers like yourself have plenty of other things on their minds, don't they? Trying to deal with lots of things simultaneously, trying to achieve the results that are expected of them and their units. So much to do, so little time, so many demands.

Easy to see how the high maintenance people can become a pain.

It's a good moment to preview some of the talented people's remarks that we will cite in the next section. For instance:

◆ *'I think organizations want pseudo-talent but really legislate out the real thing . . . most organizations reward political talent, but innovative people tend to be boat rockers.'*

◆ *'I want to work where bright, talented people are at the top (rather than seen as "problems").'*

These were not isolated remarks in our research.

Time for a more elaborate statement of the point by one of the managers who contributed his thoughts and insights to our research. It's another provocation, but it points to the tension that lies at the heart of managing talented people.

Most companies do not actually want talented people

I have worked in different companies of various sizes in the City and have observed how 'talented' people have fared. These are my personal views.

I think 'talented' means someone who is original and creative and constantly questions things. These people are extremely difficult to manage – they are easily bored and refuse to accept the authority of the boss just because he is the boss. This is why most companies, despite all their propaganda, actually do not want talented people. They say they do because publicizing this indicates what a modern, creative, vibrant corporate culture they have and also because if they only want talented people in their company, and they are the management of this company, it confirms their own belief that they themselves are talented.

What management in business really need lower down the company is not talent but very competent people with an extremely high boredom threshold. Can you be truly 'talented' and a good corporate lawyer, accountant, or investment banker? No way, the work is far too boring for anyone with a really enquiring mind. The recruitment preferences of these companies confirm my view. Many firms engaged in graduate recruitment for instance look closely at O and A-level results. Why? Because O and A-levels are all about rote learning and self-discipline, not talent. [One of the world's most famous consultancy firms] apparently have a marking system for judging CV applications. They give more marks to degree subjects like physics and engineering than to history and literature because they are 'harder'. Don't they mean, more 'boring' and less requiring of imagination and truly analytical thought?

Whatever talent there might be in the lower reaches of the company is crushed anyway by corporate culture by the time they get to the top of the company. As Nigel Nicholson of the London Business School says: 'There is a global dearth of people who really have what it takes to be significant agents of change. The trouble is that corporate culture kills off these people before they can climb the ladder. It's usually the safe people who manage to get to the top.'

Companies definitely need talent at the top of companies to design and implement new and competitive strategies, but they know deep down that lower down the company they don't want talent but people who can do a job well and won't be troublesome. How do they deal with that contradiction? How do they create the talented board members of tomorrow?

Best of luck for your book . . .

Well that is quite a note to end the section on. About time we heard from the talent themselves.

Before we do let's just expand the managerial definition of talent to include the underlying expectation of creativity, even if at times managers' behaviour seems to contradict this.

Talented people are those expected, by their managers, to produce superior performance both now and in the future through the application of their creativity.

talented people's expectations

Having heard from the managers, it is time to listen to what talented people say about their expectations. In the course of preparing this book, we spoke to many talented people, people identified by others as being talented, superior performers. That's what managers say they are looking for. So what are these talented people looking for? The answer has to be part of the definition of talent.

We asked them three questions:

1 What are the essentials that you look for from an employer?

2 How do you want to be managed?

3 What will you not tolerate?

The answers are remarkably consistent. But we'll let them speak for themselves, by quoting some examples.

What is talent saying?

Here's the first. She's from California.

1 I look for innovation in an employer. I look for creativity and mental energy, a desire to do things differently. I look for an egalitarian environment, small size because usually you get more flexibility. I want something highly informal where I can work my own hours, dress as I please, figure out my own role. Cutting edge, leading edge in market position, product offering or employment practices. I look for good opportunities for advancement and reward.

2 I want freedom and autonomy. I work best in an unstructured environment where I can find my own level, explore, add value. I want to be supported and mentored but with a fairly hands-off style. I want to be understood — the value I might contribute, something about the vision I see. It's terribly frustrating when people 'don't get it'. Now, that doesn't mean that every idea that spews out of my mouth is fabulous, but it would be bliss to work with people who can expand and develop them — or at least understand the direction of my thinking. It's also heaven to have someone who can operationalize things — have the ideas, work them through to see if they're viable, then hand them off. My most comfortable level will always be somewhere around vision and strategy and problem-solving, much less around day-to-day running of things. Also, some kind of career path, reward, recognition that doesn't require highly developed political skills. I see so much mediocrity in organizations, from people whose only real contribution is that they fit the mould perfectly.

3 What I won't tolerate: stupidity, mediocrity, cowardice, poor business practice. 'This is the way it's always done around here.' Suffering fools gladly, doing dumb things badly because that's the way they're done, not be able to change things, not being able to make a difference, have an impact. Lots of politics, rewarding a**holes who are bad managers but look right but offer little else. Not being recognized for what I am good at, having to do things consistently that I don't do well. I can do all of the above for a while and then I quit the job.

Unfortunately, these requirements don't sit too well in the corporate structure. I think people with these predilections probably end up in R&D, self-employed, writing, consulting — something like that. In many ways, I think organizations want pseudo-talent but really legislate out the real thing – again, depending on what you mean by talent. Overall, most organizations reward political talent, but innovative people tend to be boat rockers.

Here's the second. She's from Ireland.

1 What do I look for from an employer? The essentials:

 ◆ corporate values/culture conducive to innovation;

 ◆ bright, talented people at the top (rather than seen as 'problems'), role models;

 ◆ intellectual stimulation and opportunities to learn new stuff;

 ◆ strong appraisal and feedback system;

 ◆ loadsamoney – not quite, but recognition through remuneration.

2 How do I want to be managed?

 ◆ objectives set and left to get on with it;

 ◆ mentored rather than managed at a detailed level;

 ◆ in an open and honest environment.

3 What won't I tolerate?

 ◆ drudge and lack of stimulation;

 ◆ too much politics – hard to define this, but I don't want to spend my life dealing with undercurrents and egos ... just want to get on with the job;

 ◆ dishonesty – based on recent experience, it's one of the most demotivating factors I've ever encountered;

 ◆ lack of feedback, both positive and negative ... another killer.

Here's the third. He's English.

1 What do I look for in work?

◆ creative collaboration: the chance to work on better and/or new ways of doing things with others;

◆ personal differentiation: an opportunity to stand out as offering something different or, if possible, unique;

◆ engaging colleagues: people who share a view that it is possible to do something better by working well together.

2 What would I look for from my manager?

◆ a lightness of touch: steers which help to avoid pitfalls but which don't especially 'direct';

◆ to recognize the value of innovation: new & different = 'good';

◆ encouragement to 'have a go': take some personal risks in support of personal and business development.

3 What will I not tolerate in an employer?

◆ poor leadership: inability or unwillingness to listen; playing the 'I am the boss' card to halt debate; solution or sell driven style; bullying; selfishness; cult of personality; claiming solutions as his/her own.

Hearing any themes in all this?

Let's turn the volume up a bit. Let's amplify it. Here are the responses from three more people. Two of them are British, one is from New Zealand. They've all worked internationally. We'll let them take one question each.

What are the essentials that I look for from an employer? I want to work somewhere that you are empowered to pursue your ideas. Because you want to do something a bit extra-ordinary. And when you get that chance, it's kind of scary, but it's great. Because I want to take things on. I want to use my skills. I want to make a contribution to a bigger cause. It's important to me to work for an employer who respects what you want to contribute, who takes the trouble to find out what my goals are, where I'm coming from and where I want to go.

And someone else . . .

How do I want to be managed? At a distance. To be given some guidance rather than direction, to be asked to 'give this some thought', or told 'that idea won't work here because . . .' with some explanation of why it won't fit the circumstances. So, given feedback that is very real, very direct, very grounded in the situation that I'm working in. Not patronizing. No time wasted on flattery and obfuscation. That way it saves me time and it teaches me something.

And finally . . .

What won't I tolerate?

◆ lies and bullshit! I'd rather know where I stand even if it isn't great news;

◆ my point of view not being taken into consideration;

◆ backstabbers and those who only care about their own career and not those they manage;

◆ working for a company which consistently seems to be a step behind its competitors;

- ◆ working for a manager who thinks you are fantastic one day and the world's worst employee the next!

- ◆ being told you won't get promotion due to the short length of time you have worked in the firm – ridiculous!

These are my initial thoughts; let me know if you need anything else!

Hmm . . . Some food for thought here, eh?

What makes talent tick?

So what is the pattern in what talented people are saying? What are the recurring, underlying messages? What makes talent tick?

Talent is urgent. That's the message.

Because, when you listen to the voice of talent, you can hear its urges:

- ◆ an urge for personal growth
- ◆ an urge to be on the move
- ◆ an urge for the here and now
- ◆ an urge for meaning and purpose
- ◆ an urge for agency and choice
- ◆ an urge for self-respect
- ◆ an urge for fun.

Ignore these urges at your peril. They underpin the expectations that talented people bring to the relationship with their employers, to their day-to-day dealings with their managers. Managing talented people is about providing challenges that can match and utilize these urges. That's not an easy task.

Talent is urgent. It needs your urgent attention.

Talent is complex. Talented people are neither robots nor mindless fireballs. Managing talented people requires an understanding of talent's expectations and how these relate to managerial expectations. Understanding that can then serve as the basis for the more difficult task of balancing these expectations in practice. To do this we need to understand the urges and expectations of talent in greater depth.

So let us elaborate our explanation of the urges, illustrating what they signify. Also giving you an opportunity to recall your own experience of them, because recognizing the urge is the first step towards being able to discuss it.

The urge for personal growth

'What do I look for from an employer? Intellectual stimulation and opportunities to learn new stuff.'

'The perfect manager would be somebody you could use as your mentor.'

Talented people want managers they can learn from, managers who will be generous in directing them to others from whom they can learn more. Having a job to do isn't enough for talent. Talented people will pour themselves into a job, but they need to regard that job as an opportunity for development. Talented people will gladly work for others, but they need to believe that those others have something to offer. You can't just be the boss for a talented person. Position isn't enough. You've got to be a boss with something.

In effect, talented people are saying:

◆ Just being older or having been here longer isn't enough to make me respect you or accept you as my leader.

◆ Don't expect me to continue working for you, unless I'm developing as a result of the relationship.

- Luke Skywalker is eager to learn and wants to work with Han Solo as well as with Obiwan Kenobi.

Talent is asking:

- What can I learn from you?
- What can you teach me?

Do you recognize it? The pressure to be supported to do a part-time MBA or some other Master's degree, for example. Catch your own example below

The urge to be on the move

'I want to be passed high-profile opportunities in order to develop my current role.'

'I need to take things on, things that other people might be reluctant to do, things that will help the team to better itself.'

Talented people don't just want personal growth for the sake of it. They do want personal growth for its own sake, but that's not all they want. They want the chance to use that growth. They want new and bigger challenges. They want to use their talents. They want to keep moving.

Talent is saying:

- Don't give me the 'jam tomorrow' speech.
- What you call progression, I call standing still.
- Don't expect me to be prepared to mark time.

There is often a restlessness about talented people. They are not always clear about where they want to be going, but they know that they want to be on the move.

So talent asks:

- What's next?
- What new challenge can you give me?
- Why can't I do that now?

Recognize the urge? The pressure to be seconded to a high-profile project or to be given charge of a particularly important task.

Have you got your own example?

If you're having difficulty managing talented people, don't delude yourself into thinking that you can just keep your head down and wait till the whirlwind has moved on. Talented people don't behave like that. They want to be in the moment as well as on the move . . .

The urge for the here and now

'I won't put up with lies and bullshit! I'd rather know where I stand, even if it isn't great news.'

'I want a strong appraisal and feedback system. I won't tolerate lack of feedback, both positive and negative. That would be a killer.'

'I want to get stuck in and do more than my fair share!'

Talented people don't like to waste time and they hate other people wasting it for them. They want to get on and make things happen and that means they like to be in the action, in the here and now. Which is a messy place, full of problems and possibilities, tangles and tensions, complexity and politics. It's a challenging place, this gap between the idea and the outcome, and talented people don't leave it be. They get in about it and expect others to be doing the same.

Talent says:

◆ Get on with it! Straight talking, please.

◆ Let's do it!

◆ I want to deal with that.

Management is in the moment. That is certainly where past performance and future expectations meet, or collide.

Talent is asking:

◆ So what's the problem?

◆ What's going on?

◆ What are you saying?

Recognize this one? For example, when your patience wears thin because your star player wants to spend time getting personal feedback, while all you want to do is press on with the task in hand.

And your example . . .?

Talented people can seem impatient and demanding. And they are. But not without reason . . .

The urge for meaning and purpose

'What am I looking for from an employer? Cutting edge, leading edge in either market position, product offering or employment practices.'

'I see no point in working for a company that consistently seems to be a step behind their competitors.'

Talent is not purely individualistic. It wants to be part of some bigger purpose. It wants to *lend itself* to some bigger purpose. Talent doesn't want to be on the move just for the sake of it. Talented people want to do things that are significant, go to places that matter, get involved with ventures and communities that are worthy of their effort and attention.

Talent is saying:

◆ I want to make a difference in an organization that makes a difference.

◆ I want to be going somewhere in an organization that is going somewhere.

◆ I want to be working on something that matters.

You can see this at work in the graduate recruitment market, one of the most obviously competitive arenas for talent. A significant trend in that marketplace is a growing insistence on knowing about a prospective employer's values, ethical standpoint and contribution to society.

So talented people are asking:

◆ Is this undertaking worthwhile?

◆ Is this a good use of my time?

◆ What's the point?

◆ Where do I fit in all this?

◆ Am I adding value here?

You know the sort of thing. When your department is working well and your star player suddenly complains about feeling unfulfilled.

What's your experience?

Talented people are selective about where they associate themselves . . .

The urge for agency and choice

'I want to have the objectives set and then be left to get on with it. I want to be mentored rather than managed at a detailed level.'

'I need to be given space to develop my own ways to tackle jobs.'

'It was great when I was empowered to pursue my own ideas . . . kind of scary but great.'

Talented people want freedom to express themselves. They don't want their responsibilities to be closely defined by others. They seek accountability and they want to shape and develop their own roles. They like to be in the driving seat. They like to exercise choice.

They like to be in the driving seat. They like to exercise choice.

Talent says to its managers:

◆ Give me the responsibility.

◆ Let me choose.

◆ Let me decide.

◆ I want freedom of action.

We've been following a pattern here. We keep saying 'talent asks'. But it's time to break that pattern, because this urge is so central to what makes talent tick that it isn't really a question. It's a demand.

Talent is demanding, not asking:

◆ Let me get on with it.

Have you had this one yet? When, far from seeking your advice on how to solve a problem, she barely remembers to let you know that she has sorted it . . . and you worry that your own boss will think you're out of touch. That's just one example. What about your own?

Talent likes to take responsibility, to be personally resourceful and to be able to be self-sufficient. This doesn't necessarily mean that talented people don't like to work with others . . .

The urge for self respect

'What won't I tolerate: stupidity, mediocrity, cowardice, poor business practice. Not being recognized for what I am good at.'

'It's got to be an open and honest environment. I won't tolerate dishonesty. Based on recent experience it is one of the most demotivating factors I have ever encountered.'

'I had eight interviews when I joined this organization and only one of those people bothered to ask me what I had done in my previous job.'

Talented people want to be treated as individuals, not numbers. They want to be listened to and heard. Talent wants to be treated with respect, but don't expect it to whine if it isn't. Don't expect talented people to spell it out for you, if you are failing to treat them with respect. They have far too much self-respect for that. Talent sets and monitors its own standards and will act as it sees fit and necessary to respect itself.

Talent sets and monitors its own standards and will act as it sees fit and necessary to respect itself.

Talent says:

- ◆ I won't do a role if it doesn't make me feel good about myself.
- ◆ I'm not selling you my soul!
- ◆ I'll be the judge of the value of what I'm doing.

Talent is asking, and it won't ask you:

- ◆ Do I feel good about what I'm doing?
- ◆ Do I respect myself working here?

This is a tough one because the signs tend to be more indirect. Clues only. Such as when your star player becomes either unusually tight-lipped and withdrawn or volubly critical of others, to an unusual degree.

When have you seen this?

Oh, and by the way, in case you're thinking that they sound particularly solemn, intense and robotic . . .

The urge for fun

'I won't tolerate drudge and lack of stimulation.'

'I can do the job, fine, but the problem is I'm not really enjoying myself.'

This is an intriguing part of talent's complex set of expectations. Talented people don't seem to have a particularly high need for others. In many ways they tend to be self-sufficient. But at the same time they often exhibit a high need for stimulation, for novelty. Other people can be an important source, but it seems to be the stimulation rather than the people that matters to them. This is a theme that will come up again, when we come to unpick some of the particular challenges of managing talented people.

For the time being, just make a note of what talent is saying.

- Have fun.
- Life's too short. Don't be boring.
- Next!

And these other questions that talent is asking itself, often unconsciously.

- Am I enjoying this?
- Are these people stimulating to work with?

Here's an instance. When you've taken them to a high-profile meeting and they come out with some inappropriate use of humour that has you cringing with embarrassment in anticipation of the later remark, 'I thought he was one of your best?'

What have you seen?

Corroborating evidence

Perhaps you're thinking that it's all very well for us to make these assertions about what talent expects. All very well for us to quote a few people and claim that they are typical. All very well for us to tell you that this is the pattern that we discern from working closely in this domain and listening carefully to many people over a number of years.

We hope that our analysis of the urges will have resonated with your own experience. That it will have helped you to find words to describe your own observations. But perhaps you haven't seen these things. After all, that is one, and perhaps the biggest, source of problems in human systems, the failure to notice what is happening.

So where's the supporting evidence for our reading that talented people have a complex set of expectations?

Good question. And it's good to have a healthy level of scepticism. Good also to be open to persuasion in the face of the evidence.

Like this . . .

The Career Innovation Research Group is a joint venture that was brought together in 1998 *'in response to the worldwide shortage of talented young professionals'*. The group comprises eight multinational companies and is facilitated by Whiteway Research International, a careers research consultancy based in the UK. The partner companies are intentionally from diverse sectors: BAE Systems (the former British Aerospace), Cap Gemini, Freshfields, Marriott International, PriceWaterhouseCoopers, Reuters, SmithKline Beecham and UBS. And there are many other contributors to the group's research, including AXA Group, Ben & Jerry's, Cable & Wireless, Canon, Compaq, Diageo, Mobil Oil, Motorola, Reebok and Unilever.

The group's 1999 career innovation survey, *Riding the Waves: The New Global Career Culture*, explored the career values of a large, international sample of young professionals. Peter Capelli, Professor of Management at the Wharton School, reckoned that because *'the new generation of professional is demanding a different relationship with its* employers', this report offered *'an excellent starting point to understand how to get and keep them'*.

OK, so much for its credentials. What does it reveal?

It identified the following values as significant to its respondents:

◆ wide horizons

◆ work–life balance

◆ professional expertise

◆ challenge

◆ autonomy

◆ social environment

◆ meaning

◆ power and influence.

And, importantly, it revealed that *stability* was not an important career value for young professionals.

Recognize the similarity between these headings and the urges that we have been describing?

But it is one thing to recognize these issues at a headline level. It is another to be able to manage the challenges that they present on a day-to-day, week-to-week basis. We need to get below the surface, because you, as a practising manager, need to get below the surface. We need to recognise the implications and consequences of the expectations that talented people bring to work with them.

But surely, you may be thinking, that's what we were doing when we spelled out what talent was saying and prompted you to ask yourselves whether you were responding to the urges of talent.

Yes . . .

But . . .

Talent can be double-edged

Are talent's urges a good thing?

Come on, you're a manager. You're expected to make judgements. (Sorry to sound like some interrogational quiz-mistress.) What do you think?

One easy answer is that in themselves these motivations are neither good nor bad. They just are. Urges. They're there. In different strengths and combinations for different individuals, but typical of talented people as a whole.

Hmm . . . doesn't really get to grips with the issues, does it?

Another easy answer (that is to say, one which sidesteps the tricky bits) is to say, *'Yes, I want my people to be ambitious, impatient, eager to learn, keen to progress. I want them to respect themselves and to demand stimulation.'* All the right phrases.

But do you really want that? Or to be more precise, do you really want the behaviours that go with that, the demands on your time and attention, the pressure to make opportunities available, the possible murmurings from other people about inconsistency of treatment, the clamour, the occasional overstepping of the mark?

Here's how one of the managers we consulted describes talented people. It illustrates the double-edged nature of talent's urges rather neatly, we think.

High impact, but high maintenance.

Certainly easily bored.

Easily impatient with other (less talented) colleagues.

Restless innovators – driven by a dissatisfaction with the way things are (OK is never good enough) and a type of laziness ('Isn't there a quicker way?').

Require a big purpose (beyond financial targets) to really motivate them.

More temperamental because they care about it. Take it personally.

You rarely see talented people doing jobs they don't like (even if they're more vocal about the organization's shortcomings).

So, are talent's urges a good thing? Yes and no. They mean that talented people are motivated and that's helpful. But they also mean that talented people are particularly sensitive to whether their expectations are being satisfied. And that's more of a challenge.

What's the essence of the challenge?

Often it comes from a tension between what talent wants and what management needs. And that tension can easily emerge, because urges are just that, urgent. They're not docile. They strain at the leash. So, from a managerial perspective, each of the urges has a downside as well as an upside and it is easy for that downside to become apparent.

Consider . . .

The upside of the urge for *personal growth* is that it makes for diligent and effective learners. As a manager you want people who are committed to learning. These are the people who make sure that the same mistakes don't keep happening, who can take on more responsibilities and get more done.

But the downside is that an urge for personal growth can lead the individual to overemphasize learning at the expense of performing. When they want to give their attention to developing their capabilities for the future, you may just want them to concentrate on achieving in their existing job, using their existing knowledge and skill set.

The upside of the urge to be *on the move* is that it makes for people who are willing and eager to take on challenging assignments. As a manager you want people who are prepared to volunteer, to put themselves forward for the difficult tasks and projects. There's usually more than enough for you to cope with personally, after all!

But the downside is that this urge to move on to the next challenge may leave you feeling that they haven't paid you back for the investment of time and energy, training and attention that you have had to give them bringing them up to speed in their current role.

The upside of the urge to be in the *here and now* is that it makes for people who will inject immediacy and pace into what they do. As a manager you want people who are in the moment, getting to grips with the realities of the situation. You want people who are 'present' in every sense of the word.

The downside of this urge to be in the here and now can make for a tendency to be insistent. That can be useful, but it can also amount to a lack of subtlety, a lack of sensitivity, a poor sense of timing. At its worst, perhaps, it makes for impetuosity. And we've all seen examples of what can happen when someone raises an issue too bluntly or without enough empathy.

The upside of the urge for *meaning and purpose* is that it makes for people who think about the bigger picture, who ask the 'why' question. As a manager you want people who are going to perform mindfully. You want people who can make sense of what's going on and then make use of that sense in a purposeful way. People who can think for themselves. (Incidentally, we know from our own research that this is a characteristic which is particularly important in facilitating transition from one role to another, a recurring challenge for the talented. So in that sense it's a very good thing!)

Is there a downside to this urge for meaning and purpose?

Yes, in principle there could be, if what you need is a bit of mindless conformity, some thoughtless compliance. That might be what you're looking for from all your people. We hope not. If that's what you want from your talented people, you're probably not making best use of them.

The upside of the urge for *agency and choice* is that it makes for someone who wants to take responsibility. As a manager you want people who are prepared to be accountable. We've all met plenty of people who would rather duck and dive, the teflon-shouldered. You also want people who are in the habit of developing choices and evaluating consequences. These are the ones who can take on the business of turning ideas into action without getting stuck in a single way of looking at the challenge.

The downside of this urge for agency and choice can be a failure to involve others when they're needed. The super-hero complex! The superior performer who is accustomed to achieving great results largely through his/her own efforts . . . who is then put into a role where the contribution or co-operation of others is essential, and who then struggles to share the responsibility for achieving results, preferring rather to drive him or herself into the ground rather than admit any sign of personal dependence.

Get off! It's *my* football!

The upside of the urge for *self-respect* is that it brings a strong sense of personal values. As a manager you want people who are self-aware. It lightens your load when it comes to giving feedback or appraising performance, if you're dealing with people who have a clear sense of standards and how they are stacking up against those standards.

The downside of this urge for self-respect, from your point of view as a manager, is that values are essentially personal. Individuals have their own and increasingly these are not inherited, from organizations, parents or other authority figures. In our experience talented people, in particular, are much more likely to have values and a sense of self that is personally defined and thought-through, rather than shallowly derived from someone else. And that is where much of the challenge of managing talented people can start. At their worst they may be simply too individualistic, too self-referential, to work effectively within the inevitable confines of an organizational context. At the very least you have to expect that talented people will not simply accept your organization's norms for how people should be treated. They will have their own views on how that should be, and how they should be treated in particular. And, as their manager, you're in the middle of that!

The upside of the urge for *fun* is that it makes for people who are stimulating to work with and who make work enjoyable for others. As a manager you want people who can relieve the monotony of the boring bits, because, as we all know, every job has boring bits. And we all know that there are times, when it's not boring, but the pressure is on, when the deadline is approaching and tempers are getting ragged, and the person who can lighten the mood is worth their weight in gold.

So what's the downside? Well, the urge for fun can be a complete pain when you're trying to be serious and positively dangerous when you need to be serious. You've probably seen it: the inappropriate use of humour. More typically, talented people can undermine their reputation with significant others who don't share the same urge, clients and senior managers, for example. We know one very talented financial controller who got into the habit of wearing a powder blue suit and no socks, for example, much to the consternation of auditors and prospective customers. So, what the talented person regards as a funky haircut or a piece of fashionable dressing may end up making life more difficult for them, and for you as their manager. Fun can be useful, but it can also become self-indulgent.

We know one very talented financial controller who got into the habit of wearing a powder blue suit and no socks, for example, much to the consternation of auditors and prospective customers.

So the urges of talent can be double-edged. You can't just leave talented people to get on with managing themselves. Or, to be more precise, you can't safely make that assumption. Left to pursue their own urges, even the most talented people cannot be expected to conform to organizational expectations.

In some ways they are the least likely to conform.

But we are running a risk here, a significant one. And it's time to make it explicit.

Talent is not a commodity

In seeking to draw out themes, to characterize the motivations that seem to distinguish talented people, we run the risk of treating talent as if it were a commodity. As if talented people were all alike. Like any stereotyping, this is a dangerous error.

Part – a major part – of the challenge of managing talented people is to recognize their individuality. Because individuality is particularly important to talented people. And, by definition, it is impossible to generalize about it. You need to understand what makes each one tick as an individual, case by case.

So when we describe the urges of talent, we are not offering a set of answers, but rather a set of clues. Pointers. These are drivers that seem to be common to talented people as a whole. You will still need to probe to understand how important each is to a particular individual.

And here's an added complication. You also have to probe to understand how important each is to that individual at a particular point in time. Because the overall implication of the several urges that characterize talented people as a whole is that these people are dynamic.

Not static. Dynamic. Impatient, urgent, restless. You'll need to keep up.

Don't get us wrong. We believe the primary responsibility for managing these urges rests with the talented person. We also believe that talented people would agree with us! So what's the problem?

Have you ever given much thought to the expression 'raw talent'?

Raw. Not yet developed. That's why you're managing it. When it's developed, it will be managing itself. And others. In the meantime your role is crucial.

You can't expect talent to manage issues that it doesn't recognize. You can't expect anyone to do that. And one of the things we know about 'failures' in human performance is that more often than not they are the result of oversight. It tends to be the occasion that is missed rather than the motivation or the ability that is missing.

So when your talented person is pressing for personal growth, or demanding greater freedom of action, or insisting on feedback right now, bear in mind that s/he's not doing this to be difficult. Talented people don't set out to test their managers to the limits just for the sake of it, as a form of sport. They might enjoy that as a by-product (a useful source of fun, after all) and that may well be how it feels for you, the manager, but that's not where they're coming from. What they're doing makes sense to them. They're responding to the urges of talent – as they see them.

And of course, you have to respond to the urges of management – as you see them.

No wonder it gets challenging.

And the challenge is first and foremost yours. Because, as you'll notice we never tire of pointing out, you are the manager. It's your responsibility.

So, as a manager, are you clear about what you want from talent? Because your talented people are going to be (and probably are already) coming at you to meet their expectations. What are yours? Wanting performance isn't enough. It certainly isn't clear enough, since the task that faces you is essentially one of managing a complex set of expectations, yours and theirs.

Think about it now. Before we go on. It's a good point to offer you an organizer, in this case simply some questions and some space (literally) for reflecting on them. What exactly do you want from your talented people? We know you want performance, but that's the bottom line, the lowest common denominator. You want that from everybody. We think you expect something more from your talented people.

If talent is essentially a complex set of expectations, it's time to start unpacking the expectations that managers bring to the proceedings.

What do you expect of your talented people?

Think about the talented people who are working, or have previously worked, for you.

What exactly did you expect of them?

What was the nature of their contribution?

What made their performance distinctive?

the underlying tension

So what happens when we bring these expectations together – management's expectations on the one hand, and talent's on the other?

The relationship between manager and talented person is inherently tense. This isn't a comment about the individuals concerned, although it is the individuals concerned, and the approach they take in practice, that will either amplify or resolve this tension. Nor are we saying that managers cannot be talented people themselves. After all they appeared on both our 'often talented' and 'seldom talented' lists. The point we're making is that the expectations on managers, in their role as managers, are significantly different from the expectations on talented people. They don't necessarily pull in opposite directions, but it is in their nature that they do pull in different directions.

Now of course there is a measure of overlap. Management wants performance. Talented people want the opportunity to perform. Management expects improvement. Talented people expect the opportunity to make a difference. But the extent to which these expectations converge will vary. And so will the time that they

converge. Talent is urgent, remember? It is all too easy for the expectations to diverge over time.

Being a manager is a difficult enough balancing act in any case. But when it comes to the case of managing talented people, the tensions that need to be balanced become more acute.

So how do you feel about that? Are you glad you're a manager? Are you glad to have talented people? Are the other managers in your organization glad to have them?

Because this is the hub of the issue. There is an inherent tension between the expectations of talented people and the expectations of managers. The expectations, particularly those of talented people, are complex and dynamic, and so therefore are the challenges of managing talented people.

Complex and dynamic challenges demand discerning and flexible responses. A different approach to management than the prescriptions offered in much management theory.

Making sense of a coherent management approach to talented people is the focus of the next part of this book. We present a theory of managing talented people. The aim of this part has been to reflect on the views of those involved and from it to draw a deeper understanding of what lies behind the challenge. This has provided a rich picture, to encourage your own thinking and reflections. Let's stand back to look at what we have been saying.

Reflections on managing talented people

In a nutshell:

Talent is important for organizations.

But talent is political. It is a high-stakes topic and consequently one which hinders rather than encourages open discussion. It is difficult for talented people to speak openly about their expectations.

Managers tend to define talent narrowly, in terms of their ultimate expectation, which is performance. Management definitions of talent may be less or more elaborate, but essentially reflect this prime concern rather than the concerns of talented people.

Talented people in general show a complex set of motivations, but the common theme is a need for movement, for development.

Creativity is at the heart of the concept of talent, but free thinking does not sit comfortably with organizations' need for order. There is therefore an inherent tension between talented people and their managers. This tension can be obscured to the extent that the organizational context can accommodate what talented people are looking for.

But talented people are restless and dynamic. Their relationship with organizations is inherently unstable.

At the centre of these tensions are individual managers. People like yourself . . .

We offered a definition of talent that appeared to be operating in organizations. We conclude this part of the book by refining this definition

Talented people are those expected, by their managers, to produce superior performance both now and in the future. They achieve this through urgent application of their creativity while demanding personal growth with or without the support of the broader organization. Managing talented people is the continual management of the resultant tensions underlying these different expectations.

a theory on managing talented people

This part of the book focuses on your role as manager, and specifically on what is required of you personally as a manager of talented people. Managers are already beset by an overwhelming array of advice on how to go about their roles. So our intention here is not to add to the multiplicity of demands that are already made on your time, but to highlight and explain three perhaps unobvious, but nevertheless essential impacts that your activities need to make.

You are likely to find this bit particularly valuable if you are looking for a few, clear principles for how to provide leadership to talented people and if you want to understand the rationale that explains why these principles are so important.

introduction

The preceding part of this book looked at multiple perspectives on the challenges of managing talented people. These reflections concluded by recognizing the underlying tensions between managers and talent, caused by competing expectations. Our focus now is to make sense of this, to consolidate the issues into a point of view that will provide a platform from which action can be taken. We need a theory, a principle to explain observable facts – a theory as to the role of the manager in leading talented people.

'There is nothing as practical as a good theory' – one of those quotes that has stuck with us over the years. Theories are simplified models of reality and as such can help us focus on what is important. The simplification prevents the messy nature of the actual situation obscuring the best way ahead.

That is the style of this part of the book.

The focus is on you as a manager and what you can bring to the party. It is what you have most control over (we hope) and we will return explicitly to managing the tensions in the interaction with the talented person in the next part of the book.

In the previous part we have established the view that talent has to be managed. Talented people may be superior performers, but they cannot simply be left to get on with it, even though they insist on having freedom of action. So they need attention. Special attention. Nor is managing talented people simply about stroking their egos and making sure that they have plenty of challenging opportunities. That is merely appeasement, not managing. And yet they do want, and push for, continuing personal challenge.

Talented people may be superior performers, but they cannot simply be left to get on with it, even though they insist on having freedom of action. So they need attention. Special attention.

Talented people are not easy. So you won't be surprised by our proposition that managing talented people has major implications for you and for your role. It requires a particular quality of leadership. You can be sure of this. Talented people will challenge your capacity for leadership. They may not, or may, challenge you for the role of leader. They will certainly test your qualities as a leader.

Now 'leadership', of course, is the holy grail of management literature, a concept even fuzzier than 'talent'. So this is not going to be a synthesis of what other people have to say on the subject, nor even our own attempt to scale that particular peak. Our objective here is more focused. This is because one of the reasons why the definition of effective leadership remains so elusive is that it is hampered by the search for universal principles, ingredients that will work in all circumstances. The panacea, the elixir of success, the secret of leadership.

We make no such claim.

Our interest here is with leadership in a particular context, the leadership of talented people. They present a particular type of challenge. They require a particular type of leadership. And here's the good news. By contrast with the interminable lists of leadership characteristics that you may have seen (and struggled to remember) in the past, the to-do list in this case is quite short. It's definitely mind-sized, easy to remember.

Managing talented people requires you to . . .

Alert
Enable
Inspire.

A, E, I . . . and if you want to make it even easier to remember, make it AEIOU, where O U is a reminder that it's for you to do.

Oh you!

A E I O U. The vowels. Words can't work without them. Neither can talented people.

So let's look at each of them in turn.

alerting talent

This facet of your role is double-sided. It is partly about alerting talented people and partly about alerting others to talent. (This is a theme that will reappear in subsequent sections. Being a manager of talented people often puts you in the role of intermediary, a challenging position, as we will see.)

Let's look at the less obvious task first. Alerting others to talent. Here is an illustrative episode, recounted by one of our interviewees.

Does talent speak for itself?

Now that you've prompted me to think about it, the thing that strikes me about managing talented people is that the problems tend to be unexpected.

To give you an example, some years ago I was offered a promotion. It was a similar role but on a much larger site. But you need some background first. I'd progressed steadily on my original site, and each time I was promoted I tried to fill my previous role with someone who had at least as much ability as I had. So by the time I became the HR director, the department had some strength in depth. My 'first lieutenant', who took over my previous role as employee relations manager, was particularly talented.

I think her background was in mathematics. Anyway, she was very quick on the uptake, a very clear thinker, able to see and explain the implications of proposals. And she was a good mediator. The trade union representatives had been very scathing when she was first appointed. Said she was too young, too inexperienced, didn't know anything about life on the shopfloor. They even sent a deputation to me to say they had no confidence that she could do the job. But within a few weeks, it wasn't even months, she had established a great relationship with them. It was a tough relationship. It wasn't cosy. But they respected that. She spoke to them straight and she expected straight talking back. They liked that. And she was ingenious with it, so she really got things done, sorted things out, devised new ways forward. It's always tricky when you have a change of player in employee relations, because so much hinges on the quality of the personal relationships, obviously. But in this case, after the initial short-lived concern, employee relations on the site just kept on getting more and more constructive.

So three years later when I was offered that promotion to the larger site, it seemed to me obvious that Paula, who now had a couple of very able people working for her, would succeed me as HR director. That would ensure continuity and show that the business valued talent. It was just a 'no brain' decision in my view. I just took it for granted that it would happen.

So I was more than a bit taken aback when my boss said, *'OK, where are we going to find your successor?'*

That was the first unexpected bit.

What I hadn't noticed was that although Paula's talents were obvious to me, they hadn't become obvious to my boss.

Paula getting on with the employee relations had allowed me to spend most of my time on broader business issues, in particular putting a great deal of my time into supporting my managing director in developing strategy. So he had seen a lot of me, but very little of Paula. And because the employee relations were going well, they didn't seem to be an issue. Very few issues were needing to be escalated. If they were, then I was able to deal with them. There was virtually nothing that I needed to take to the board. So Paula simply didn't have much profile with my boss.

You know the saying that 'talent speaks for itself'. Well, it doesn't. When you manage talented people, you have to speak up for them, make sure they get visibility. This was when I learned that.

And I learned it the hard way. Because when my boss asked where my successor was going to come from, it shocked me. I hadn't seen that coming.

I explained that I thought Paula was the obvious successor and explained why. He listened to me carefully. He didn't disagree. But he said, *'The trouble is, I just don't know her. And I need someone who can work closely with me, like you've been doing.'*

So he insisted on canvassing other candidates from elsewhere in the Group.

Now you can imagine how that went down with Paula!

She knew she could do the job. She knew that an outsider, however good their skills were, would take a long time to get to grips with the complexities of a context that she already understood intimately. We were a site of 2,500 people, after all. She was eager for the challenge of a director's role, and she was soon making it plain that if we didn't provide that opportunity, she would go looking for an organization that would. She had already recently turned down a couple of approaches from head-hunters.

You can see who was stuck right in the middle of all this! And stuck there for a few weeks. Because you know how long it can take to find candidates and get interviews arranged.

So there I was. On the one hand, my boss wanted me, as the existing incumbent of the job and as someone *he* trusted, to take a close part in the interviewing process with him. On the other hand Paula wanted me, as the existing incumbent of the job and as someone *she* trusted, to explain what was going on and reassure her that she was in with a fair chance. Because what was happening certainly didn't feel fair to her.

I was exhausted. By the pair of them. They were both looking for reassurance, both demanding – and getting – my time to talk about succession. Both pouring out their concerns to me. Every day, for a large part of the day, for several weeks. My big worry was that we would lose Paula before the interviewing process was over, because my boss, very properly, insisted on seeing all four candidates before making up his mind. And I didn't want Paula going into her interview and spoiling it because she was burning up with a sense of injustice.

So don't talk to me about the joys of promotion!

Actually I didn't have any time to think about my own promotion. Which was another part of the problem, because preparing myself for the new job was what I really wanted to be thinking about. So I was paying the price for making an assumption, the assumption that talent speaks for itself. It doesn't. That's part of your responsibility as a manager. You have to make sure that talented people get exposure. It's not enough that they're doing a good job and that you can see that. If you're going to hold on to talented people, give them career opportunities, especially for more senior appointments, you've got to make sure that you've given them the chance to make their mark directly with the decision-makers.

It worked out fine in the end. My boss interviewed the various candidates. Then he said to me, *'Well, it's obvious. Paula is clearly the best candidate. What are we waiting for. Let's get on with it.'*

That was an experience I won't forget.

Raising talent's profile

Talent may not speak for itself, but we hope that episode does. Failing to raise the profile of your talented people can seriously interfere with your own interests and prospects as well as theirs. Don't forget that what may be obvious to you may be far from obvious to others. It's not easy for those in the upper reaches of management to see and be aware of the talent in their organizations. It's not uncommon for senior managers to feel like Tomb Raiders when it comes to finding talent. It gets dark quickly down inside the organizational pyramid! Look out for the warning sign: when the same one or two people keep being nominated for important assignments, it usually means that the up-and-coming aren't yet on the corporate radar. It's part of your role to get them there.

It's not easy for those in the upper reaches of management to see and be aware of the talent in their organizations.

Now it's easy enough when it's in your own interests to do that, as it was in this episode. But the hallmark of true leaders of talent is that they raise their talented people's profile even when it may not be in their own interests.

Over the years we have advised a number of organizations on the establishment of succession planning and key resource reviews. A central feature of such processes is usually a forum at which the talented people are identified and discussed. Increasingly companies are recognizing that, in order to work effectively, this sort of forum needs to operate, not just at the top, but at all levels of management. So if you haven't been involved in a forum like this yet, then you can expect to be, probably sooner rather than later.

And then you'll face the challenge. Do you speak up for your talented people? Do you bring them to the attention of your colleagues, people from other departments, other parts of the business, other parts of the world? Parts of the business which might have an urgent need for talent, a more urgent need than your own. Are you prepared to run the risk of losing your talented people? Are you prepared to face up to the responsibility of acting in the wider interests? Of letting go?

It is all too easy in this context to act narrowly, to become defensive, to find some rationale for holding back. But it is a strategy that carries the seeds of its own destruction. Because its price ticket is respect, the respect of your talented people, of your colleagues and, ultimately, your own self-respect.

Don't forget that you don't own your talented people. They're not yours. They're not even the organization's. They are their own people (and, oh will they remind you, if you ever forget it!).

It may, of course, be appropriate for you to hold on to your talented people. If you believe that's appropriate, then you need to be prepared to make your case, with your colleagues and, most of all, with the talent. (Who will always have the final say. They can always vote with their feet.)

We're not much inclined to be prescriptive, to specify rules. (You've probably noticed.) But here's one.

It is never appropriate to keep talented people hidden.

Making talent clued up

Clued up is our phrase for those most able to deal with today's messy organizations. It is also a requirement of effective talent management. In fact, making talent clued up is a major part of your role.

Why?

Being clued up is the key to being personally effective. It's essential if someone wants to be successful at turning ideas into action. And that makes it an important concern for talented people, given their usual eagerness to make things happen, and given also – as we have seen – that this is one of the major expectations that others have of them.

So what is being clued up?

The essence of being clued up is paying attention to the things that matter, the particulars that will either enable or impede your ability to turn ideas successfully into outcomes. The problem is that one can't generalize about what matters. You can't give someone a list that will work in all circumstances. That's the flaw with anything that claims to provide the seven steps to success. It doesn't take sufficient account of context.

Context is crucial. One of the most telling statistics we know comes from the research which suggests that 80% of the failure in human performance arises not through an absence of ability, nor from a lack of motivation, but because the occasion to use these was not spotted.

Awareness of the needs of the moment is central to effective performance. Sensitivity to clues can make all the difference. Alertness is vital.

Situations vary and any context changes. So, to be effective, you have to keep paying attention. It's not a one-off task, it has to be ongoing. It has to be a matter of disposition.

This is the other side of alerting talent. Teaching it to be alert.

You cannot provide all the answers. No one can, so give yourself a break. Talent wants to learn, but that doesn't mean you have to be an encyclopaedia. What you can, and should, teach talented people is to pay attention to the angles that will improve the odds of understanding a context and acting effectively in that context.

What are these angles? That depends on your particular context, of course. (Pay attention!) But if you want a generic set, here are the five that we find will give you particular traction, when it comes to making sense of a context and making things happen.

- **Mind the gap** – recognize that there is a long way between every idea and its successful implementation. Crossing this gap requires you to understand it, to appreciate the territory you'll need to navigate. Ignore it at your peril.

- **Deal with the complexity** – organizations and the people within them are not simple (even if they act that way sometimes). Events interact, the impact of decisions is delayed, unintended consequences abound. Get a picture of it, generate choices, anticipate consequences and, above all, keep moving.

- **Attend to the politics** – as we have shown with talented people, valuable assets excite personal interests, and a set of behaviours to protect those interests. Effective action has to recognize these and deal with them.

- **Make your thinking GOOD** – Give it time. Open it. Organize it. Deepen it. Superficial default thinking is simply not up to the task in a dynamic world with so much at stake.

- **Make your talking action** – because talking is action. It is how things happen in organizations. If you don't have the repertoire to draw on you won't be able to orchestrate your part in the show.

The third part of this book will pick up these themes and develop them for managing talented people.

What does alerting require from you?

It is all too easy to be mean with talent, if not by design then through sheer oversight. We're assuming that, as you're taking the trouble to read this book, you're not the sort of person who would be mean by design. Not the sort of person who would feel threatened by having talented staff or seek to keep them in their place by keeping them in the dark. Such managers exist, of course. Though, you've probably noticed, they don't usually have many talented people working for them, at least not for very long.

But there is another, less obvious but equally dangerous, form of neglect. When people are talented and show motivation and capability, it is easy to assume that they don't need much in the way of support. Easy to allow your other concerns to take priority. Easy to give your time and attention to those people and problems that seem less capable of looking after themselves. An easy mistake to make.

Your talented people need your attention. Make yourself available.

You have a responsibility to your organization to alert it to its talent. You have a responsibility to your talented people to alert them to the nature of their organization, to clue them up to their context.

Alerting talent requires you to be generous in both directions. Don't be miserly with your talented people. Don't hoard your time from them. Don't attempt to hoard them. You don't own them anyway. What you have is stewardship. So your role is more like that of a financial adviser. You can increase the value of talent by calling its, and others', attention on where to invest.

It's easy to approach the role of manager from the point of control. That's the traditional angle. Making the decisions, determining the directions, controlling the resources. But, that's too narrow a view of the role of managing and it's fatally narrow when it comes to managing talented people.

Alerting the organization requires you to move out of the control mode and take the bigger perspective. You will need to broaden your repertoire of managerial styles. Move to co-operate with the wider organizational interest by sharing information openly with other managers who need talented people. Move to broach those opportunities, frankly and openly, with the talented person. Move to help them assess the opportunity in relation to their own aspirations and development. Move to broker the development of the ensuing relationships. Let go of control.

Alerting the organization requires you to move out of the control mode and take the bigger perspective. You will need to broaden your repertoire of managerial styles.

Alerting talent also requires you to take the bigger perspective. Teaching your talented people to be clued up requires you to show them how to broaden their approach too. It requires you to draw them out of their natural tendency to see things too independently, a tendency that can limit their ability to realise their potential.

Take the big view. Embrace the whole.

enabling talent

How does enabling differ from alerting?

Often alerting will be sufficient. Drawing the talented person's attention to something he or she needs to take into account, a person who should be consulted perhaps, or a useful insight into where senior management thinking is heading, or how a proposal is likely to be received. This may be all the input that's needed from you to refine what the talented person is doing. Gentle steering. What do they say about how they like to be managed? *'Supported and mentored but with a fairly hands-off style.' 'A lightness of touch: steers which help me to avoid pitfalls but which don't especially "direct".'*

At other times, however, your intervention will need to be more hands-on and sustained. As the manager you will need to take a more active part in making things happen. And again, this will put you in the middle of the action, facing both ways, trying to be an enabler both for the organization and for the talented person.

It can be an uncomfortable role, as another episode will illustrate.

A case of raw talent

I recruited Jason when he was in his early twenties. He was a graduate with a good degree and he'd been a management trainee in a public-sector organization. But he'd quickly grown frustrated at the slow pace there and that's how he came to apply to us.

I've interviewed a lot of people over the years and he was a very impressive candidate. I was immediately struck by his enthusiasm, the clarity of his thinking and his apparent willingness to challenge the status quo. That's what I was looking for. I was responsible for turning what had been a pretty lacklustre, essentially administrative function into a team that would not just support but would actively lead efforts to improve performance in the business.

So I took him on. And I wasn't disappointed. In practice he showed all the characteristics that I'd glimpsed at interview. He was energetic, incisive and he got things done. Within a few months I promoted him to a full managerial position in an important relationship management job. There were a few eyebrows raised when I did that because he was years younger than most of his peer group and some people found him a bit 'in your face' for their taste. They said he was 'a bit full of himself'. But I reckoned this was a reasonable price to pay for someone who could deliver results like he did.

So what was the problem?

Well, unexpected. It started when Jason came to me and asked for help. That was unusual in itself. The help he wanted was in making a transfer to a different part of the group. His problem was that when he had joined us, relocating over 200 miles in the process, his fiancée had expected to be able to transfer with her organization too. In fact she'd been promised a promotion that would bring her to the same part of the country within a few months. But then what actually happened was that there was a reorganization. Her promotion materialized, but it was based in the original location, so Jason decided that he needed to move back. Fortunately we had a sizeable office in that part of the world, so he wondered whether it might be possible to arrange an internal transfer.

Now this was a disappointment from my point of view, but I wouldn't call it a problem. You have to expect that your talented people will move on. That's what happens. And since you have to lose them sooner or later anyway, then it's better to 'lose' them within the company than outside it. So, although I was sorry to be facing the prospect of losing Jason sooner than I had expected, I didn't personally have any hesitation in offering to help him find the transfer he was looking for. And this other office was a busy, action-oriented place. I thought he would fit in well there.

So the prospect of letting him go wasn't the problem. Nor was it a problem securing him an interview at that other office. I'd worked closely with the managers there in the past, we'd done some successful projects together, and they were glad to meet him on my recommendation. So off he went for his interview and when he came back he was very positive, because it turned out that they had a vacancy in a similar sort of role. He'd met the managing director and one of the other directors and he thought he'd made a good impression.

The problem was that he hadn't. Or, to be more precise, he'd made a mixed impression. The managing director rang me to say that he wasn't sure about Jason. He'd seen the energy and the enthusiasm and the intellect, but he felt there was just too much self-assurance, too little willingness to give attention to what others had to say. So the managing director wasn't saying no, but he did want to talk to me about it. How good did I think Jason really was?

And that was the problem. I recognized what he was saying. I knew that this was a risk with Jason. But Jason had done a good job for me, he'd delivered results and now I wanted to deliver a result for him. I think that's an important part of managing people generally and with talented people I think it's particularly important. You expect a lot from them and, if they deliver, you put yourself out a bit more for them.

So I told the managing director that I recognized that Jason could come across as a bit full of himself, but that was because he had a lot to offer. I told him I was confident that Jason would not disappoint them.

I used my personal credibility with them to facilitate Jason's transfer. That turned out to be the problem.

Because he did transfer but it didn't work out. Opinion in the new office was pretty divided about him. Some people liked his directness, but others, particularly among the more senior people, thought he was arrogant and opinionated. Unfortunately the managing director was one of the latter. Jason stayed for a while, but when he became enthusiastic about a joint venture opportunity they weren't sorry to let him go to join the joint venture partner.

It cost me. My influence, certainly with the managing director, at that office was never quite the same again.

And the moral of the story?

I have no regrets about hiring Jason, and no regrets about helping him to get the transfer. But that was only a part of my responsibility for managing a talented person. What I recognize now is that I failed in my responsibility to take some of the rawness out of his talent. Sure, his style was helpful for my agenda at my own location. But what I should have done was to have guided him on the potential downside of that style in other circumstances. And I should have been as forceful and 'full on' with him as he was with others.

Supportive *and* challenging. That's what's required. Or in this case, with talented people, very supportive and very challenging. I didn't get the balance right and that let both of us down. That doesn't mean that Jason had no responsibility for the way things turned out. But, as his manager, I think I only did half of what I should have done.

Pause for a moment and reflect on some of the angles in that episode. We are going to come on to the issue of developing talent, but this episode also demonstrates the value of alerting talent, or more accurately the risks of not.

There was clearly an idea–action gap, the idea that Jason would take his impact in one organization with him to the next. This underplays the importance of context. The context of the first office being different from the context of the second. That had something to do with the different outcomes in each case and could have been foreseen and therefore managed, at least to some extent.

There were definitely unintended consequences of Jason's style, especially with the managing director. Could these have been predicted – probably? This would have allowed the MD's expectations to be handled before meeting Jason, his perception shaped. Possibly the course of history would have been changed.

And politics, well plenty of them it seems and a good example of the risks of staking your reputation on the behaviour of another, particularly on the talented. If you are going to do that, and we expect that you may often have to, as others in the organization seek to cover their risks (or is that their arses?), then you'd better have confidence in their abilities. You must develop your talented people.

The development of talent

Talent is not an all-or-nothing thing. But it is easy to fall into the trap of assuming that it is, particularly once an individual has been labelled 'talented'. The shine on this particular label can serve to blind as well as to draw attention. It can blind us to what still needs to be done. Because talent is not a commodity, not a condition. Talent is more dynamic than that. It can be raw. It needs to be developed.

A central part of your role is to develop talent.

So, how does talent develop?

Some of the most interesting research into this question has been done over many years by Harvard psychologist Howard Gardner. In a series of books, such as *Extraordinary Minds* (Weidenfeld & Nicholson, 1997), he reports the close studies that he has made to identify whether there are any distinctive patterns in the thinking and behaviour of extraordinary performers. These are not books that have been written for managers. Nor are many of the people whom he has studied from the world of business, although leadership is a theme that he has explored. Yet Gardner's studies are highly significant for anyone interested in talent and much of their relevance comes from the fact that they are drawn from such a wide variety of domains: politics, invention, psychology, the arts. His interest is in the nature of talent. What is it about these people that makes them extraordinarily talented?

Where does their superior performance come from? A question to command the attention of those who manage talented people.

Gardner identifies three particular characteristics that distinguish extraordinary individuals.

First, they reflect on their experiences far more than most people. Secondly, they are distinguished not so much by innate ability as by the way that they identify and exploit their strengths. Thirdly, although they fail often, and sometimes massively, they learn from these setbacks and convert them into opportunities.

Or, to turn these points into the sort of words that you will have grown accustomed to hearing us use, extraordinary performers:

1 are GOOD thinkers;

2 have strong self-awareness;

3 are assiduous learners.

Whichever language we use, these are characteristics that have strong parallels with what we call being 'clued up'. We've already established that managing your day-to-day interactions with talent needs to be done in a clued up way. Now let's look at Gardner's findings in more detail and draw out the specific implications for what you need to do as a developer of talent.

Enabling reflection

The first of the features that are, as Gardner puts it, 'regularly associated with extraordinary accomplishment', is straightforward. Reflection. Regular, conscious consideration of the events of daily life, reviewed in relation to our objectives and aspirations. It sounds simple. And in itself it is.

The difficulty is that too often we fall at the first hurdle. We just don't make time to do it. Remember our acronym? GOOD thinking. The G is for Give. Give time for thinking.

'But I don't have time.' That perennial organizational bleat. The cry of the weak. The moaning of the helpless.

Of course, time is precious. It's a scarce resource. Ultimately it's our scarcest resource. And, of course, work life is busy. We know all that. We also know that if you don't make time for thinking, then you don't move on. You make the same mistakes twice, or more. You don't spot the subtleties of what's going on. You take longer to get on top of things. Extraordinary performers don't make that mistake. They recognize that giving time to reflection is disproportionately valuable. Comparatively small investments of time in thinking can yield big paybacks.

So what do you need to do?

Encourage time for thinking. Make it not just okay but expected. One of the most successful talented people we know reports how his boss used to do just that. As a matter of routine he would make himself available for about a quarter of an hour at the end of every day for some informal ruminations on the day. The boss didn't talk much. His contributions came primarily in the form of asking a few questions. Mostly he listened. He 'held the space'. The talented person recalls how much, for his part, he came to look forward to these few minutes at the end of the day, when he could 'collect his thoughts' and 'put things in perspective'. What he particularly valued was the space it gave him to think.

Sounds trivial. But it isn't. As a manager you can be enormously influential in how your people spend, or waste, their time. Providing time and space for reflection is a simple contribution that you can make. And one which is of particular value for your most talented people. Because they will tend to make good use of it.

How do you do it?

Just do it. You don't need to go on a course. Simply make some time. It doesn't need to be particularly long. It's more important that it's regular. A disposition to reflect. Don't permit the time to be interrupted. Make it a feature of your style, the way you do things. And protect it. That's the way to convey the message that it is important.

Otherwise it will tend not to happen. We know people who work in project roles which, by their nature, require a great deal of reflection, thinking through complex situations and variables. Yet even they report a sense of guilt if they catch themselves staring out of the window, while they are deep in thought. Even though they are not gazing at the view, but are immersed in their thinking, they say that it often makes them feel uneasy because, in appearing inactive, they do not appear to be doing what is expected of people at work.

That's the strength of the absurd, but all too prevalent, idea that thinking is not a valuable form of action. For superior performance, thinking is action. Mindful action is more valuable than mindless activity.

For superior performance, thinking is action. Mindful action is more valuable than mindless activity.

If you want to ask some questions that will prompt people to reflect, try these.

◆ What's been happening?

◆ What's on your mind?

◆ What are you puzzling over?

◆ What strikes you as significant in what's been going on today?

It's not hard to come up with questions that will prompt reflection. What people usually find harder is just staying in that reflective mode long enough to let the fruits of the thinking emerge. The temptation is to rush to make sense of things, to judge and evaluate too quickly. Reflection, on the other hand, requires pondering, wondering, turning things over, looking at them from different angles, considering alternative perspectives.

So conspicuously encourage, and enable, your talented people to reflect. And 'hold the space' for them to do it.

One of the reasons that reflection is so powerful is that it brings the lessons from experience to the surface. It enables us to articulate them. And that helps us to apply them. People often claim to have learned a great deal from experience and yet, when you ask them to tell you exactly what they have learned, they cannot do that. They are vague. Fuzzy. (Default thinking strikes again!) And that leaves the learning locked up, hard to access except in a re-run of the circumstances in which it was originally acquired. When it tends to be triggered by the familiar circumstances.

But that's not much help when you're no longer in the same situation. And the problem is that talented people tend not to linger in familiar circumstances. They are on the move. They look to find themselves in new situations. And organizations like to get value from the people they see as talented. So they like to put their talent into new situations. Got a new challenge? Throw your best people at it! It's a well-worn managerial formula.

But have you ever wondered why people you thought were talented fail so often in these circumstances? One reason is because they can't transfer what they learned from their previous experience into the new situation. It's in them. But they haven't fully made sense of their previous experience. Literally, they can't articulate it. Until they do, making use of that experience is bound to be pretty hit-or-miss. And it's in the nature of new challenges, situations that are unfamiliar, complex, and dynamic, that you can't just rely on past experience. You have to figure your way through. Talented people, perhaps more than most other people in organisations, are the ones who will find themselves in the situations that need GOOD thinking. That's why enabling reflection is such an important part of your role.

Talented people, perhaps more than most other people in organizations, are the ones who will find themselves in the situations that need GOOD thinking. That's why enabling reflection is such an important part of your role.

If you want to read some more about being reflective, then have a look at the work of an international authority on thinking, another distinguished Harvard researcher, David Perkins. In his book *Outsmarting IQ: The Emerging Science of Learnable Intelligence* (Free Press, 1995) Perkins lays out a compelling range of evidence to support his argument that reflective intelligence can not only be learned and developed but is the basis for more effective performance in challenging circumstances.

It's not impossible to teach yourself reflective intelligence. But, it's easier if someone helps you. One of Perkins' most telling points, it seems to us, concerns the importance of actively supporting the development of the individual's thinking and capacity to think for himself/herself. *'Intelligent behaviour is not characteristically the solo dance of a naked brain, but an act that occurs in a somewhat supportive physical, social and cultural context.'*

As a manager you have a unique contribution to make through creating and maintaining that 'somewhat supportive' context for your talented people.

Enabling strong self-awareness

Let's turn to the second of Howard Gardner's characteristics of the extraordinarily talented. And to his finding that it is not so much their level of capability as the facility to recognize and make use of their strengths that distinguishes them. Note the phrase, recognize *and* make use. Self-awareness only becomes valuable when it is applied.

That's why we've called this section enabling strong self-awareness.

How do you do that?

Again, the answer is not complicated. First and foremost, you enable strong self-awareness by giving feedback. Feedback that enriches the individuals' understanding of themselves. And in the case of talented people, in particular, you need to give them an understanding of what makes them different from others, how that can be valuable and what limits its usefulness.

There is plenty of readily-available advice on giving feedback. If anything, there tends to be too much advice on it. Books, courses and videos where you sink under the weight of all the things you are supposed to remember about how to give (and receive) feedback effectively. All that stuff about the 'right' environment and balancing your remarks and so on.

But remember what we saw, and heard, in the first part of this book. Talented people put great store by feedback. They want it. (Unlike many people.) And they want it to be in the moment and to the point. No bullshit! No word games. So don't overcomplicate things. You don't need to and talented people won't thank you for over-elaborating the process.

But do make your message clear. So, keeping our advice mind-sized, here's how to construct your message. In three parts:

1 observation

2 implication

3 modification.

First, tell them what you have observed about them. Give them the evidence. It is often said that this is to make your comments credible. And that's true. But it's also about enabling the other person to recollect the situation that you're referring to. Remember, talented people are in a hurry. They tend to have a lot going on. You need to help them to call to mind what you're talking about.

Secondly, spell out the implications of what you have seen them doing or heard them saying. This is the heart of feedback, the unique contribution that only the observer can provide. An external perspective on their impact, the effects and consequences of what they have done. An angle that the do-er does not have. They might be aware of it. But they might not. Often they are not, because there is so often a gap between the intention and the impact. This is where you really contextualize and develop someone's understanding of their performance.

Thirdly, offer a constructive alternative. Or two. Or three. But the key word is *offer*. The trouble with telling people what they should do is that it tends to provoke a reluctance to do it. That's true for most people, but especially the case for the talented ones. They're accustomed to working things out for themselves, remember? They tend, as we've already seen, to be creative and independent-minded. Not the sort of folk who usually take well to being told, but adept at exploring and developing possibilities. So offer your suggestions as possibilities. They're more likely to be heard. And acted upon.

Okay, this three-step process does not just apply to talented people. It is one that applies to the giving of any feedback. We offer it here, not just because good feedback-giving skills seem to be rare, but because talented people in particular will test your skills in this area. They will solicit feedback and, if their talent is to be developed, they need to get it. As a manager you owe it both to them and to the organization to be skilful at giving feedback.

So much for the process of giving feedback, but what about the content? At one level, of course, only you can answer that. It depends on the individual concerned and on your particular context. So we have to leave that detail to you. But at a broader level, we can offer you some useful guidance on the sort of content that talented people are likely to find particularly helpful. Again, it draws on Howard Gardner's findings. One of the features that Gardner noticed about the extraordinarily talented was something he called 'fruitful asynchrony'.

Eh?

Yes, that was our first reaction too. What he means is a tendency for talented people to turn to advantage the ways in which they differ from others in their particular time and domain. Recognizing what it is about them, their background, upbringing, experience, interests, skills, that makes them different from most of the other people around them. Different from the norm. This is clearly a basis, if exploited, for making a distinctive contribution. Distinctive does not, of course, necessarily mean useful or successful. But it might. It has that potential, especially if one looks for ways to make difference useful, to use it to add value.

What he means is a tendency for talented people to turn to advantage the ways in which they differ from others in their particular time and domain.

Think for a moment about the extent to which organizations need diversity. Take a classic example, teamworking. It's well known from the research on what makes teams effective that a variety of roles need to be filled: the ideas-generator, the co-ordinator, the catalyst, the critical judge and so on. Think also about the extent to which organizations depend, in fast-moving and competitive market environments, on being able to differentiate themselves from their competitors. Case made, we would suggest, for the importance of diversity.

And case made also for the importance of you giving your talented people feedback that enables them to understand what it is that is different about them. Their opportunity to make a distinct and additive contribution. The sooner they can see that, the sooner they can make it the subject of their reflections. And the sooner they can leverage it. Both for their benefit and for the business.

A simple piece of enabling talent, provided that you do what talented people do, and give the matter some reflection. So that you can give some quality feedback. And provided also that you actually take the trouble to do it.

Because it may involve trouble, not just time. There is risk as well as value involved in encouraging people to be different. (It's that old tendency for risk to be associated with reward.) But let's stay with the theme of enabling talent. Let's look more closely at Gardner's third tendency of the talented, and at how you, as a manager, can cultivate it.

Enabling assiduous learning

Even before we start to explain this bit, you will probably have noticed that there is a strong link connecting the three distinguishing characteristics of the extraordinarily talented. They are all to do with mindfulness, with taking time to think and using that time to think about things that can differentiate performance. Reflection is the engine. Self-awareness is one of the fuels. Drawing from experience is the other – which we call learning.

Reflection is the engine. Self-awareness is one of the fuels. Drawing from experience is the other – which we call learning.

Gardner notes that his own findings are corroborated in this respect by others' research. In her book *Gifted Children* (Basic Books, 1996), for instance, Ellen Winner observes that the 'exceptionally bright' show 'a rage to learn', exhibiting outstanding energy, curiosity and focus in relation to the subjects that interest them.

Energy, curiosity and focus. Some resonances here, we would suggest, with the urges of talent that we described earlier in the book.

The late Michael Howe, a British researcher into the exceptionally able, found a similar pattern of intrinsic motivations underpinning their performance. He found that they:

◆ have a very strong sense of direction, and independence;

◆ tend to be sharply focused on particular goals and aspirations;

◆ resist distractions and avoid getting side-tracked;

◆ usually work very hard to acquire the capabilities they need.

He concluded that beneath the apparently effortless exterior, exceptional performance is based on immense determination, concentrated attention and sheer hard work.

All of which sounds thoroughly desirable from a corporate point of view, until you recall that talent's direction and goals may be at variance with the ones that you, as their manager, are expected to achieve. So it won't come as a surprise to hear Howe also noting that these qualities can make exceptionally talented people 'seem eccentric and difficult to live with'.

So we come back to the tension at the heart of managing talented people. They are highly motivated, but these motivations may pull in a somewhat different direction from the one to which organizations want to harness them.

This is one of the reasons why, as a manager, you cannot simply leave talented people to take charge of their own learning. They will take it. They have the 'rage to learn'. But in what direction will they take it?

This is where the concept of self-directed learning runs aground in an organizational context. As a humanist philosophy it is unarguable. Respect the individual. Encourage their growth and development. As a managerial philosophy it is delinquent. Let's get real. In a business context we want people's learning to be relevant. The high-sounding principle, to which too many managers have become wedded, that it is up to the individual to take responsibility for their own learning, is both lazy and negligent.

So your enabling role has an organizational dimension too. It is not just for the benefit of your talented people. Not just about giving them time to think and self-awareness for its own sake. It's not just about clearing obstacles on their behalf. It is also about directing their learning. Directing with a suitably 'light touch', of course, but steering it nevertheless. Talent will provide the assiduous bit. You may need to direct that energy.

Which brings us back to the findings of Howard Gardner. The critical feature that he discerned in talented people's learning was its framing.

'Framing . . . the capacity to see not so much the bright side of a setback as the learning opportunity it offers – to be able to take what others might deem an experiment to be forgotten as quickly as possible and instead to reflect on it, work it over, and discern which aspects might harbor hints about how to proceed differently in the future.'

Construing experience in a way that is useful for future performance. This is another distinctive contribution that you can make as a manager of talented people. It's somewhat like encouraging reflection, but more focused, and also more directive. So you would go beyond offering a few prompting questions and would contribute a combination of focusing questions and opinions. Such as . . .

◆ What have you learned from that experience?

◆ What sense do you make of what happened?

◆ What has that taught you about how things work round here?

◆ What has that taught you about how to get things done round here?

◆ Let me offer you another way of looking at that.

◆ Let me outline some of the choices and run through the pros and cons.

◆ Let me suggest some of the consequences and repercussions.

◆ How could you use what you've learned?

◆ When is your next opportunity to use what you've learned?

You are not just leaving your talented people to make their own sense of what has happened. You're getting more directly involved in the learning process than that. Providing a supportive environment for their learning, but also a challenging one. Hearing how they 'frame' their experiences and putting forward alternative ways of interpreting it.

To illustrate, here's one of our favourite episodes from researching this book. It comes in two parts, because it was one of those rare opportunities to hear first hand both from the talented person and from the person who manages them.

Framing talent's energies

The talented person speaking about her boss:

I'll tell you what he's really good at. When I'm throwing a strop. You know, when I burst in to see him because I need to let off some steam. It's usually because something isn't happening that should be happening. Something getting in the way of a project that I'm trying to put forward. Perhaps someone who promised to do something by a certain time and hasn't. You know the sort of thing. And I get frustrated when other people don't seem to care as much as I do. So I go to see him and often it's to tell him that I can't put up with any more of this, and it's certainly to throw my teddy out of the pram for a bit. And what he's really good at doing is listening, even when I'm in a mood, and saying things that somehow change the way I'm thinking about it all. I don't quite know how he does it. But I do know that I come out with a clearer sense of purpose and feeling that I'm not wasting my energy after all.

Now, what has her manager been doing? Here's his side of the story, in answer to the question: have you evolved or observed in others any smart ways of dealing with the challenges of managing talented people, ways of channelling their ability with maximum effectiveness and keeping them fulfilled without their leaving? (Snappy little question, huh?)

I turn as many objectives as I can into 'missions', often framing goals in more personal terms (be the best rather than beat that target ... crush the competition rather than take market share) ...

Tell them as much as possible about the big picture, and include them in as much decision-making as I can.

Remove as many bureaucratic obstacles or mundane legwork as I can from their path – focus them on high-impact stuff.

This is reframing in action. It gives talented people a wider and more constructive sense of the possibilities open to them. But notice also how it works with the grain of talent's urges, the urge for personal development, the urge to be part of a bigger purpose, the urge to be creative, the urge to make a significant contribution. Remember also what we have seen repeatedly, talented people tend to see things from an autonomous angle. This is the downside of being so independent-minded. It can make them over-rely on their own framing. Reframing of thinking is therefore one of the most powerful contributions that a manager can make to enabling talent. Reframing redirects and refocuses talent's energies rather than allowing them to turn into accelerated frustration.

So, to answer the question that we posed at the beginning of this chapter ... Enabling talent is like alerting talent, but demands a more forceful, a more challenging intervention on your part.

Reframing redirects and refocuses talent's energies rather than allowing them to turn into accelerated frustration.

Your role in enabling talent requires you to be actively drawing it out from its natural predisposition to be too independent, too autonomous, to see things too narrowly from its own point of view. Don't just leave it alone. Your task is to ensure that talent gives more consideration to the organizational perspective and to the views of others. Which means you being less detached. Not an observer and commentator, but in the action, where the tensions are most apparent. Working with those tensions.

inspiring talent

This sounds like a tall order. Surely we expect to be inspired by the talented, not to have to inspire them? And how does the need to inspire people with talent square with our earlier proposition that you don't have to motivate them?

The answers to these questions are perhaps best reached by considering another question first.

Where does talent go?

It's an important question, because talent tends to disappear. The talent wars are not just about increasing competition for a key resource. There is a process of attrition at work too. There is the obvious disappearing, when talent leaves your organization and goes to work somewhere else. But there is also the unobvious disappearing, where the person remains but the talent vanishes. Or at least becomes much less evident. Have you ever noticed for example how the 'talent' label tends to be applied to the young much more often than to the middle-aged? Partly this is because there is more time left in the young, and therefore 'more' potential, at least in a strictly quantitative sense. But partly it is because 'talent' can fade. The talented can lose their distinctive edge.

Why is that?

We've looked at a variety of characteristics that seem to distinguish the extraordinarily talented. Creativity, independent-mindedness, a disposition to reflect, strong self-awareness, the ability to make a virtue out of being different, assiduous learning.

What happens to these characteristics over time? And, in particular, what tends to happen to them in the specific context of business organizations?

They can become corroded. It's not inevitable that this will happen. But there are strong pressures that tend towards it happening.

The reason is, as we've pointed out elsewhere, that work can be a hostile and threatening environment. It's certainly a political one, a place where personal interests are competitively championed. It's also an environment where the accent is on achievement, where people are quick to evaluate, quick to judge each other, quick to criticize. That's the nature of the territory and it's a nature that can serve to blunt talent.

In the previous chapter we wrote about the value of enabling talent by making talented people aware of what makes them different. We stressed the importance of diversity. And we stand by that. But let's look at the other side of that coin. Let's not be naïve. There are strong pressures to conform in organizations. The pressure not to be different. The pressure to stick to the procedures. Not to make a judgement call. Not to take a risk.

These are real pressures. That's why people who buck the rules – and get away with it – are so often held up as heroes in organizational mythology. You know the stories: the guy who goes far beyond authority and charters the helicopter to get the package through, to the delight of his customer. The story is potent simply because it is so rare. How commonly do people really stick their necks out like this, even on a much smaller scale? How much more common is it for people to keep their heads down, as the risks are going up, particularly in an age which has demonstrated that there is very little security of employment, almost regardless of personal achievement?

We've seen opinion survey evidence from management populations where as many as 97% have expressed the belief that saying what you really think can damage your career prospects. An extreme example perhaps.

But only perhaps.

Do you remember the managerial dilemma that one of our interviewees so starkly pointed out?

'Companies definitely need talent at the top to design and implement new and competitive strategies, but they know deep down that lower down the company they don't want talent but people who can do a job well and won't be troublesome. How do they deal with that contradiction? How do they create the talented board members of tomorrow?'

Dealing with that contradiction is your job. It's an essential part of your responsibility of enabling talent, for ensuring that the flow does not dry up. Even though it will require you personally to stand in the middle of that contradiction and absorb the pressures that it generates.

Which can be tough. But also inspirational.

Here's another short episode that we've collected, to illustrate the point.

Backing talent

Anton was bright, creative, ideas driven. He was personable, mature beyond his years. He was in his late twenties but had the interpersonal skills of a late thirty-something. And he was culturally challenging.

What happened was this. We were running a recruitment campaign. Anton was given the job of searching for and selecting 'bright young things' for the business. Part of the process involved an external advertisement campaign in the national press. He worked with the agency and produced some very imaginative and witty copy. Culturally, it was very different. And it was risky.

He presented his ideas and was asked to tone them down. They were just too far out. But he went ahead anyway. Questions were asked in head office!

I asked him why he'd ignored what he'd been told to do and gone ahead regardless. He replied that he believed his approach was in the best interests of the business and that he would defend this position wherever he needed to. He was aware that his approach had been iconoclastic. He enjoyed that!

He had put me in a difficult position. But I did what I believed was right. I supported him publicly, despite the criticism. Between ourselves I told him that since it was his decision, he had to live with the implications of that decision. That meant he could front any further defence of it, if it came under any more scrutiny. Which it did. And he defended it admirably, pointing out that the approach could hardly be criticized at a time when the business at corporate level was calling for culture change!

And the moral of this story? Back the judgements of your talented people, even when you think they're wrong or need some adaptation. Even if you need to take some flak in the process.

Taking personal risks

So how do you inspire talented people?

By personal example. By standing up to the pressures towards conformity and compliance that organizational life generates. By many small acts of personal courage which show that it is possible to be different, and to remain true to yourself and your values in an organizational context.

Because in the absence of this sort of example, talented people become disillusioned and then they check out, either physically or psychologically. If they don't actually leave the organization, then the things that gave them an edge become blunted.

Here's another episode. It's from another talented person, someone whose career has taken him from manufacturing shopfloor to board room in an organization with an international reputation for excellence.

I've worked for both sorts of manager. The ones who inspire you are the exceptions. But they do exist. They're the ones who are prepared to attempt things that others wouldn't dare to try. They see what needs to be done. They check it out with people too. They're not afraid to be told they're wrong. But when they go for it, they stick with it. Through thick and thin. And there's plenty of that. There is always plenty of opposition that comes out of the woodwork when the going gets rough. The inspirational ones are brave. They don't settle for the quiet life. They behave like real leaders. They say what they believe. They'll tell their boss if they think he's talking nonsense. And they'll explain why. When everybody else is nodding in agreement to what they know to be a ridiculous timescale, the inspirational manager is the one who stands up against the 'groupthink' and says that it can't be done by then. But they'll also commit themselves to when they will deliver. They put up with the ridicule that gets thrown at them, the boss who sneers that maybe they're not up to the job and the so-called colleagues who join in because they can scent a bit of blood in the water. They stand up for what they really believe, even though they know it's not going to be popular. And, in my experience, they usually turn out to have been right.

And I've worked for the other sort, the ones who do not have the courage of their convictions. That's not leadership. And you just don't respect them as people, never mind as leaders. When they think they might be in trouble or that there might be some criticism coming their way, they turn on their own people. It's not just that they palm off any blame that might properly be coming at them, it's more basic than that. They just don't address the issues. I've noticed this very often with people who reach the senior level jobs in their organizations; they start to become much more concerned with protecting their own position and taking the line of least resistance, and much less interested in delivering change and improvements in the business. I wasn't prepared to go on working with someone like that. That's why I left.

It destroys talent. I say that because I honestly believe that most businesses lose a huge number of talented people. It happens because when they are still quite low down in the organizational hierarchy, they don't see this stuff. Or they don't see it at first hand. They are shielded from it by the levels. But when they get close to it, they find they're working with people whose values they just can't respect and whose behaviour doesn't even seem ethical. So as they progress upwards in the company talented people become more disillusioned rather than more excited and committed. No organization is going to be a winner in the talent wars unless it has leaders with courage and personal integrity.

When to be inspirational

So, what sorts of situations present you with the opportunity to inspire talent, to keep it excited and committed and as sharp as it can be? You need to spot these moments, as and when they arise, so that you can use them. When you need to. In the moment. Because the opportunities are in the moment. They are fleeting. Hesitancy is seldom inspirational.

You usually get at least one tell-tale clue for free. It usually comes in the pit of the stomach.

Actually these moments are not so hard to recognize. You usually get at least one tell-tale clue for free. It usually comes in the pit of the stomach. Because the opportunities to inspire generally arise in the situations that make people anxious. Such as . . .

◆ when the stakes are high;

◆ when a decision is risky;

◆ when the outcome is uncertain;

◆ when blame is flying;

◆ when you disagree with the majority;

- when your proposal will entail additional cost (never a guarantee of popularity);
- when others are being negative;
- when you might lose face;
- when someone else will lose face;
- when disagreeing with someone more senior;
- when it might damage your career prospects;
- when a previous judgement is being called into question.

We're sure that you can illustrate this list from your own experiences. What you might find even more valuable is to think for a moment about when one of these opportunities is next likely to come along. So that you can be sure of taking it, when it does.

Why be inspirational?

Why exactly does inspiring talent matter so much?

Because one of the implications of the research into what makes people 'talented' is that it is learnable. Think about the findings we have already outlined.

Reflection.
Learnable.

Independent-mindedness.
Learnable.

Awareness of one's strengths.
Learnable.

Assiduous learning.
Learnable.

The framing of experience.
Learnable.

Being talented is learnable. And for that reason the stock of talent need not be limited. As a manager in the talent wars, one of the most potent contributions you can make is to grow your organization's pool of talent. At the very least you have to protect what is already in the pool. And this is why it is doubly important that you seize the opportunities to be personally inspiring. Because these opportunities are greatest in precisely those situations which present the biggest threats to learning.

When blame is flying. When criticism might emerge. When face is at stake. These are all factors that militate against assiduous learning. Because learning is hard work. It requires application and effort. It needs sustained attention. It doesn't just happen. And it requires individuals to put themselves at risk. Because learning means doing things differently, and this requires an acceptance of personal responsibility. Which might, and in fact often does, also entail shouldering some criticism. So potential loss of face and self-esteem are also involved in learning. No wonder learning is fragile in the world of work.

That makes it part of your role to make it easier for your people to learn. It is especially important to do this for your talented people, because, as we have seen, assiduous learning is at the heart of what makes them extraordinary. You need to find a way to create an environment where it's OK to learn, where learning is not undermined by the sense that it is an admission of weakness or failure or incompetence.

You need to find a way to create an environment where it's OK to learn, where learning is not undermined by the sense that it is an admission of weakness or failure or incompetence.

Now we know that plenty of managers pay lip service to the concept of the learning organization. But we also know that in business performance is a higher priority than learning. Sure, learning will be acknowledged as important. But, when the chips are down, business values performance over learning.

It's another of the natural tensions of organizational life that managers need to handle.

Unfortunately, although many managers have had some exposure to the idea of the learning process and of learning styles, these concepts are both concerned with how people learn. They start from the assumption that people want to learn. But if learning feels personally risky, as it often does in organizational life, then we need to know what maintains a person's disposition to learn and continue to learn.

Far fewer managers know much about that.

One person who does, however, is American psychologist Carol Dweck. Again, she is not from the world of management. But she has studied learning and learners for over 20 years. She has found a marked and highly significant dichotomy in the mindset that people bring to learning.

On the one hand, there are those with what she calls the 'entity' mindset. They exhibit 'helpless' responses to setbacks. That is, they tend to lose sight of past successes and to amplify current failures. They become excessively self-critical and lose faith in their intelligence. They become negative and show little persistence. They become unco-operative because they see peers as competitors for self-esteem. Their learning becomes inhibited and their performance deteriorates.

On the other hand, there is the 'incremental' mindset. People with this frame of mind think and behave very differently. In the face of setbacks they maintain a 'hardy' response. They don't get drawn into blame, but remain optimistic, not unrealistically so but inclined to the belief that a way forward can be found. They persevere in the face of obstacles. They recognize that mastery will take time and effort and they maintain their willingness to invest that time and effort. They think carefully about their performance, continuously monitoring, re-examining and redesigning the strategies that they are using. They remain co-operative because they value collaboration. Their learning remains robust and their performance improves.

Those are the choices. What sort of people do you want in your organization? It's a no-brain question.

Now here's the really intriguing bit.

It would be wonderful to be able to say that talented people all show the incremental mindset. Certainly Dweck's research suggests that the dichotomy is very marked. Her subjects tended to polarize, either entity or incremental. They are either one or the other. But her studies have, to our knowledge, concentrated specifically on students, a wide range of them, from early in education to university, but all students. Do you see the same polarization in people when they get older, when they find themselves in the world of work?

Not exactly.

All we have is anecdotal evidence. We have not conducted formal research studies in this area. But describing the symptoms of the entity and the incremental to people at work, principally people in professional and managerial roles, we have found that the two mindsets have strong resonance. The indicators are readily recognized. However, even talented people consistently report that they find themselves moving between the two, rather than holding either one or the other. Specifically, they make the point that it can be hard to stay in the incremental frame of mind at work, and very easy to fall into the negativity of the entity mindset.

Specifically, they make the point that it can be hard to stay in the incremental frame of mind at work, and very easy to fall into the negativity of the entity mindset.

And they are clear about the circumstances that tend to tip them into the entity mindset . . .

◆ when the stakes are high;

◆ when a decision is risky;

◆ when the outcome is uncertain;

- when blame is flying;
- when you disagree with the majority;
- when your proposal will entail additional cost (never a guarantee of popularity);
- when others are being negative;
- when you might lose face;
- when someone else will lose face;
- when disagreeing with someone more senior;
- when it might damage your career prospects;
- when a previous judgement is being called into question.

Recognize the situations? Understand the importance of being personally courageous in these circumstances?

Learning is central to being talented. An incremental mindset is fundamental to assiduous learning and continuing effective performance. But the incremental mindset is difficult to maintain in situations where past successes tend to be discounted while current shortcomings are amplified, and where judgements are acutely personal. As they are in cultures, such as Euro-American-style business cultures in particular, which place high value on individual achievement and the individual is so often made to feel to be competing with peers for recognition.

In fact, the whole managerial concept of 'talent', of being a key resource, of being on the 'high-fliers' list or 'gold-rated' may reinforce an entity rather than an incremental mindset. And so become self-defeating. Because it values performance over learning. The 'better' schemes are recognizing the importance of learning, even if labelled differently, say as adaptability. This isn't too surprising as it follows logically from the managerial definition of talent, discussed in the first part of this book, that talented people deliver superior performance now *and in the future.* The requirement for future performance presupposes an ability to adapt to new circumstances. The ability to learn.

However, there remains a dangerous irony in talent lists. The belief is that praise and recognition encourage further performance. But Carol Dweck's research suggests that praising those with high ability can be counterproductive, because it can promote fear of failure self-doubt and poor coping with setbacks.

Spotting the danger signals

The point we have been driving at (or pounding, you may think) in this discussion of entity and incremental mindset is not just that motivation can fluctuate, but that the consequences can be far-reaching. Even, perhaps especially, for the people you have identified as your talent.

So what exactly are we asking you to do?

◆ Be alert for signs of the entity mindset.

◆ Enable and encourage the incremental mindset.

◆ And do these things for yourself as well as for your talented people because your example matters enormously.

Here are the real danger signals.

◆ Signs of 'learned helplessness', a state of mind which is produced when experience shows no reliable or consistent pattern of outcomes to the actions one has taken. Ever had that feeling cross your mind? Ever had it stick there? It produces the expectation that whatever you do, it will turn out to be ineffective. And it becomes self-fulfilling. Accompanying clues include withdrawal, passivity, lack of responsiveness. If you sense these things persisting in any of your talented people, there's no point shrugging it off as them being 'a bit down.' It's time to help them back into the incremental mindset.

We'll explain how in a moment. But first some other danger signals.

◆ Fear of failure. When there is a great deal at stake, people can become tense, nervous and anxious. Not trying, or limiting the effort put into the task, can then emerge as a defensive strategy to cope with the fear of failure. It's a natural human reaction in a high stakes situation. It serves to protect the self-esteem, but it also stops people making the most of their talents. As Michael Howe pointed out, *'It takes an unusually self-confident person to see that failing is just an indication of the level of performance achieved at a particular moment, rather than as a sign that one has somehow failed as a person.'*

◆ Fear of success. Eh? Yes. People can become anxious about the consequences of success, for instance because it can be the prelude to a promotion or a change of role and consequently greater risk of failure. We know one very talented occupational psychologist who was promoted on the strength of his outstanding performance and later actually requested to be demoted because he believed he was more capable in his previous non-managerial role. Another reason behind fear of success is commonly the fear of an associated social rejection. Like the worry people often have about losing friendships when they are promoted over their former peers.

There is no evidence that the talented are immune to these concerns. On the contrary, there is plenty of evidence that they can become prey to self-doubt which undermines the effective development and deployment of their capabilities.

In summary, in providing inspiration the manager of talented people needs to be like the pacemaker, the runner responsible for setting a demanding standard from the start of the race, the person who must provide leadership, although only temporarily.

Is this an accurate metaphor? We tested the idea with an athlete who runs for Cambridge University (a likely place to find some talented people). This is what she told us. (Thanks, Grace.)

The pacemaker benefits the other runners by helping them to achieve new personal best performances; without this additional pressure it is unlikely that self-motivation alone could produce winning results. But the pacemaker has got to be someone the runners respect, someone who shows they know what they're doing, setting a pace that's stretching but achievable, who is in touch with you even though you're behind them. Good pacemakers know what's going on for the other runners; they watch the shadows and listen to the breathing; they know if someone is keeping up or if they're feeling unsure and will adjust if necessary. They pull superior performance out of you both by showing you where to adjust your effort and mentally, by giving you a sense of the possible and helping you to think your way through the race.

O, U ... Oh you!

The manager of talented people is not a manager. Not a conventional one, anyway. To manage talented people you need to be, and be seen to be, an individual in your own right.

Be yourself. *'To thine own self be true.'*

Up till now we have been stressing the need for you to draw talent out from its natural independent position. Now it's time to join them, where they're coming from. To demonstrate your own independence. Because, if you don't, you won't win their respect. You won't inspire.

There are several reasons why it's up to you, as a manager, to inspire talent.

Talent needs to learn. Talented people hunger for learning. They need it not only to grow their talent but even to sustain it. Organizational life often discourages learning. It takes energy and courage to be an assiduous learner at work.

Talented people like to pursue opportunities. Not all opportunities work out smoothly. Actually, most of them don't. Most involve setbacks and difficulties en route. It takes energy and courage to pick yourself up, dust yourself down and start all over again.

Talent is often about making a difference by being different. Being different is risky. It can make someone a magnet for any hostility, criticism and blame that's going around. And there's more than enough of it going around in most organizations. It takes energy and courage to go on being different.

Talented people are ideas people. They like to put ideas into action and, not surprisingly, they are often idealistic. The idealistic can become disenchanted by some of the grim realities of organizational life, or just by its ordinariness, by people who seem dull or slow, uninterested or self-interested. It takes energy and courage to be both idealistic and realistic.

Talented people are ideas people. They like to put ideas into action and, not surprisingly, they are often idealistic.

Talent depends on strong self-awareness. Yet increased self-awareness can serve to highlight the extent to which one is out of place in a particular context. It can amplify the sense of being mismatched. It can accelerate the decision to move on rather than stay and grapple with the tensions and the dissonance. It takes energy and courage to be yourself.

Being energetic and daring comes easily to talented people. They have those urges. But maintaining energy and daring is hard work. You can't expect talent to have boundless reserves. And beware of the circular argument that runs, 'Well, if they were really talented, they wouldn't run out of these qualities, therefore they can't be talented after all.' Being a manager who shows energy and, especially, courage will not guarantee to sustain these qualities in talented people. But it will certainly improve the odds. In your favour. And theirs. And your organization's.

A, E, I, O, U

If that is what it takes – how well are you doing at the moment?

The next part of this book is designed to help you make use of our reflections and the sense made here of the challenges. It will look at the specifics of developing your capabilities to deliver, to manage the tensions of differing expectations.

To set the scene here is a short questionnaire, an inventory of your capabilities to manage talent. You can use it to focus your attention on your own development and use it as a checklist summary of this part of the book.

Make an assessment of the degree to which the statement is true of you and your approach to managing talent – where H is high, M is medium and L is low.

	H	M	L
Alert			
I know who my talented people are			
I keep comprehensive information on my people			
I share the capabilities of my talented people widely			
I understand how my company manages talent			
I make time for my talented people			
I am willing to let my talented people move on			
I talk politics with my talented people			
I help my talent get their ideas into action			
I help talent focus on the important things			
Enable			
I take an active role in the development of my talent			
I know my talent's strengths and weaknesses			
I provide time to help my talent reflect on their experiences			
I help my talent exploit its unique strengths			
I frequently offer feedback			
I encourage time for thinking			
I redirect the focus of my talent when they get stuck			
I use prompting questions to improve my talent's thinking			
I guide learning towards the needs of the organization			
Inspire			
I stand up for my talent			
I take risks with my own credibility to support my talent			
I lead by example			
I absorb the pressures of organizational contradictions			
I openly disagree with my boss			
I help talent maintain a positive outlook when disappointed			
I would describe myself as courageous at work			
I look out for signs of self-doubt in my talented people			
I am myself at work			

Make a note of the other things you do to alert, enable and inspire:

As you look back at the questionnaire, what sense do you make of your pattern of answers?

the practice of managing talented people

This part of the book provides a practical approach to the day-to-day challenges of managing talented people. Although the challenges can present themselves in a confusing variety of forms, there is a pattern below the surface. Once you can see this pattern, it becomes a useful framework for action. We provide a series of perspectives which build into a thorough approach that will enable you to keep proceedings to the point and to manage your interactions with talented people, and other interested parties, more effectively.

You are likely to find this part especially useful if your primary requirement is for clear guidelines on how to proceed or if you are looking for readily applied tips on how to go about managing talented people.

classic problems

Before offering the practical advice we need to understand what we are getting into. First let us consider some of the 'classics'. What do the challenges of managing talented people look like in practice? What are the sorts of situations which the managers of talent find difficult and demanding? Try making a list. It will probably look something like this . . .

The Ultimatum – where the talented person, knowing his or her value, uses the prospect of leaving or taking up another job offer to bargain for something he/she wants.

The Prima Donna – where the talented person makes an exceptionally valuable contribution in certain regards, but at the same time consistently manages to upset other people in the process.

The Runaway Enthusiast – where precocious talent oversteps the mark, exceeds its authority and drops you in the mire.

The Fussy Eater – where talent becomes 'picky' about what it will and will not do, selective about the tasks that it will take on.

Moments of Obscure Brilliance – those occasions when a talented person with a reputation for creativity and innovation comes across as simply unintelligible, but still leaves you with the uncomfortable feeling that there is something important in what he or she is saying.

The Shadows of the Limelight – where a talented person starts 'stealing' the credit, perhaps because successes come to be attributed to the talented person regardless of his/her actual contribution. It can leave others, including yourself, eclipsed and less influential.

The Poachers – when other managers come, often under cover of darkness, to try and lure talent away from your team.

The Lynch Mob – where others come to complain to you about what they perceive as the favouritism being shown towards the talented person.

The Victim of the Egalitarian – where your ability to create a developmental opportunity for a talented person is blocked by another manager's refusal to acknowledge anyone as talented on the grounds that it is unacceptable to be elitist.

The Fallen Star – where talent encounters a setback, fails to live up to its anticipated potential or to deliver against expectations.

Ten situations that are not unusual in the vicinity of talented people. Situations that present practical difficulties and challenges for the manager of talent.

Many management writers would proceed at this stage to provide advice on how you should handle each of these scenarios. If you find yourself in Situation A, then apply Solution A, and so on. In our view, this is the equivalent of treating managers as if they were rats in a maze and management writers were the all-seeing experts whose task is to educate them into recognizing the shape of the maze and the most efficient routes through it.

Wrong on both counts (although managers may often feel as if they are in a maze and writers may be prone to deluding themselves into believing they are omniscient!).

We do not pretend that we can offer you a definitive list of the situations in which you will find it challenging to manage talented people. There are certainly more than the 10 we have listed here. We do not have a comprehensive map of the maze, for the simple reason that there can't be one. The territory is too special for that. There are many interested parties, with different interests, shifting and changing over time.

We do not pretend that we can offer you a definitive list of the situations in which you will find it challenging to manage talented people. There are certainly more than the 10 we have listed here.

You can't buy a map for this sort of territory. You have to make it for yourself. And you have to do that on the move, as you work your way through the territory, your particular part of the territory.

We can't give you your map. But we can teach you something about map-making, about the sorts of features to look for and the nature of the relationships between them. We can, and in this part of the book we will, help you to see the patterns below the surface of the challenges of managing talented people. That will give you a clearer sense of what's going on. And that in turn will give you the basis for making informed choices about what to do.

the nature of the challenge

Managing talent is principally about aligning expectations. (If you haven't read our explanation for that assertion, you'll find it in the first part of the book.) Management's dominant expectation is that talent will deliver superior performance, while talent itself is looking for personal growth. Both parties acknowledge the needs of the other – well, sort of – but essentially each has a different dominant focus.

So if aligning expectations is the central challenge in managing talent, what are the key features of the task?

Well, we think the features make this a special problem, in fact S.P.E.C.I.A.L., that is:

Shared
Political
Emergent
Complex
Individual
Active
Live!

Sorry if you have just reached for the nearest paper bag, acronyms are not for everyone. Just another device for keeping challenges mind-sized.

What exactly do we mean by S.P.E.C.I.A.L.?

Shared

The psychologists of the world might describe this problem as being 'embedded in the social system' (yes, we know they/we should get out more). That is, it does not solely lie within any of those involved; it exists between them. The challenge of managing talented people is not owned by a single person, but is the responsibility of all those it touches. The quality of the relationship between you as the manager and them as the talent becomes central.

A consequence of this is that if there is an issue, it would be wrong to place the cause of it at either party's door. It will have grown up between you. Often this is the product of a series of interactions, some direct, some indirect, that grow over time. That conversation by the water cooler, an e-mail, the last pay award, a comment from another manager, all build the character of your relationship. It is truly a shared creation.

If the problem is shared, so must be the solution.

Political

Politics are the 'deliberate efforts made by individuals to use power in pursuit of their own particular interests', according to Cranfield School of Management's David Butcher and Martin Clarke in their book *Smart Management* (Palgrave, 2001). Political behaviours are most evident around scarce or prized resources, as people compete, and use such power as they possess, to secure their share.

Political behaviours are most evident around scarce or prized resources, as people compete, and use such power as they possess, to secure their share.

Talent, by definition, is both scarce and prized. By the organization, by you, by itself. Talent is also powerful. One of the recurring themes in our conversations with people was that talent 'gets things done'. It uses its influence to get others to do things they would otherwise not have done. That is power.

The stakes are high with talent. Managing talented people is a political challenge.

Emergent

First psychology, now philosophy. A property of a system is emergent when it arises out of the simpler, lower-level component parts of that system, but is not predictable from those components nor reducible back to them. In other words, the emergent features are genuinely novel aspects of such systems. Or more simply, the whole comes to more than the sum of its parts.

Thinking about organizations and about people is often stuck in a quite 'mechanical' mindset. The world is imagined as if it were a machine, one that can be deconstructed into a set of parts that, if understood, explain the whole. While our intuition tells us that it isn't like that with people, we often behave, particularly as managers, as if it were. Management is stuck in the mechanical metaphor.

You will not be able to reduce the issues of managing talent to a set of neatly interlocking components. It isn't like that. Unforeseen and unpredictable issues will emerge from a combination of seemingly unrelated factors. So expect the unexpected!

Complex

Emergence is one of the features of complex systems. Managing talented people is a complex challenge. In managing people we are particularly referring to 'dynamic complexity', that is the interplay between things over time. It is particularly important to remember this when thinking about how to deal with the problem. It is too easy to associate with what might be called 'detail complexity' which is related to scale, the volume of issues to deal with. The solution to that kind of complexity, detail complexity, is to analyse more, to go deeper, to map it all out. While deeper thinking is a good thing, this is static analysis and relying on it risks masking the dynamics of the situation and consequently making it harder rather than easier to manage.

The solution has to be dynamic too. Managing talent means interacting with talent. And talent is often impatient. Managing talented people is about making sense of what you can, and then making use of that, iteratively. Keeping on the move.

Individual

No two people are the same. No two situations are the same. There are no simple formulae. Talented people in particular tend to have a strong leaning towards individuality.

The good news is there is no wrong way to do it. The bad news is there is no right way to do it. Beware of simple or universal prescriptions.

Active

Dealing with talent means doing things. It's an active process, not a passive one. This is a consequence of the features we have been describing. You have to learn as you go. Learning involves thinking and reflecting, making sense of what is happening, but it also involves doing, applying your thinking, making things happen.

Talent won't let you stand still anyway. It is urgent.

Faced with complexity and politics it is tempting to sit back, to wait, to be cautious. No! You have to keep moving, keep acting and interacting. It is the only way to make sense of what is really going on.

Make sense. Make use. Make sense. Make use. Make sense. Make use. Make sense. Make use . . .

The mantra for managing talent.

Live!

Oh and if all this wasn't enough – it all takes place in real time. This is live TV. No rehearsals, no chance to fluff your lines and do a retake.

You got one shot, baby. You better take it!

One of the implications is that you need to be adept at recognizing these features. In the moment. In the course of your interactions with talent. Because that's where you have to manage these things in practice. And of course, they don't come neatly labelled. That's the trouble with live action. It's fast and messy.

So here is a short episode, to give you some practice in spotting what is going on and to illustrate the features we have been describing.

An episode in the life of talent

I knew about Dominic. Not much, but his name would come into conversations from time to time. He was one of our rising stars, brought in to manage one of our teams and had been quietly making an impact ever since.

Our paths had crossed directly once. Our parent company ran a global MBA programme and Dominic had been to see me to discuss how appropriate it would be to his development. He was also sounding out if we would support his application. I remember it as a good conversation. I found Dominic mature, thoughtful, clearly wanting to make a difference, but still working on how. It was an open, straightforward discussion.

My main focus at the time was a major organizational change, designed to increase customer focus and reduce operating cost. I was pleased when Dominic was selected for a key role, a significant promotion. All the more surprising when, a month or so later, he resigned. He had got a place on a full-time MBA programme and was sponsoring himself through it.

What happened? This is how Dominic described the situation.

'I had spent 10 years in the same line of business. I had experienced increasing responsibility, but really the nature of the work hadn't changed. The scale had increased – I was managing more business, more people. But I had no more authority. My scope for influencing the direction of the business, for decision-making was pretty much the same.

I was excited by the reorganization. I saw the opportunity for more access to senior management. I was looking forward to their investment in me. I had spent too long being policed rather than managed, I only saw my manager when it went wrong!

I remember being called in to meet with the heads of the division. "We are making you a director – well done." I was delighted and I asked an obvious question, or at least it seemed obvious to me – what is expected of me? I was shocked that it seemed to take them by surprise. I wanted to know what meaty challenge they wanted me to tackle, but the dialogue just didn't happen.

I had been thinking about an MBA for some time. Over the previous few years I had watched our management team fall apart in response to external changes in the market. They didn't know how to respond. I didn't want to become like that. I wanted the toolkit to deal with this kind of problem. I could see our business moving into a new age. We had been dabbling with electronic media and I wanted to know how to find the right strategy to exploit it.

At a basic level, I was really bored. I wanted to broaden my life. My partner works in the same industry. Our friends do too. I was becoming a narrow person. I needed to break out.

I really wanted to do the MBA and it felt like this was the only window. If I didn't do it now, then I never would. It was a big risk. It comes at quite a cost, both financial and personal. My preferred route would have been a completely new challenge at work, perhaps supported by a short course or two. But when even a major promotion seemed to just bring more of the same, I knew it was time to take the leap.

The company reacted well. They have given me financial support, which validated my decision. I have a project to do in return. It is good to have a tangible thing to do, but it feels like going backwards. I have changed, but I am not sure others want to see it.'

So, what did you notice? What sort of indicators were there that this was a S.P.E.C.I.A.L. situation?

Shared: the recurring issue of support, for instance.
Political: the feeling of 'being policed', the 'personal and financial risks'.
Emergent: 'It seemed to take them by surprise'.
Complex: the range of issues and 'They didn't know how to respond'.
Individual: Dominic's specific agenda: the MBA, how to exploit electronic media, his feeling that 'I was becoming a narrow person'.
Active: 'The company reacted well'. But re-acted, you'll note.
Live!: 'I needed to break out'; 'Time to take the leap'.

We are sure you can spot other features too.

This is a simple tale in many ways, but it's a good illustration of the nature of managing talented people. Let us draw your attention to a few particular themes that seem to us to be particularly significant in this case:

◆ Expectations not matched – 'What do you expect from me?', asks Dominic.

◆ The interactions – between Dominic and the current senior managers, but also the historical relationships that influenced his decision.

◆ It is not fully captured in Dominic's narrative, but we are sure you can imagine the political manoeuvres behind the scenes. The retrospective sponsorship possibly serving as a face saving device for the managers involved, implying 'we meant to do this all along'.

◆ The importance of personal growth, that is not just satisfied by organizationally bigger roles.

◆ The emergent nature of the outcome – not even Dominic's preferred option.

That is the nature of the territory. In the next section we will get into what you can do in practice to work your way through it.

what is 'practical advice'?

Having established the nature of the territory, how can we help you to navigate it?

This is a question we have spent a long time arguing out between ourselves. Practical advice is almost synonymous with simple answers. How else can it be practical? Yet, once you accept the fluid and personal nature of the issues, what use are prescriptions? They become trite generalizations. Our resolution has been to stand back from the specific problems and to look for a process that can be flexible enough to capture the subtleties of the situation and yet still be easy to remember and simple to use.

Our approach to managing your talented person has three elements:

1 seeing clearly what is happening;

2 understanding what each of you want;

3 delivering on it skilfully.

Sounds too easy?

Well, you'd be right to think that. It isn't that easy. We have invested so much time and energy (both ours and yours) in describing the nature of the task for that very reason. The real rub is that within this simple process you need to act in real time – you have to improvise.

Improvisation requires you to hold on to the big picture, the 'story' of what is happening, while drawing from your own repertoire of inputs. As we all know, the secret of great (improvised) comedy is timing. The same applies here. It is the art of reading what's happening in the story (seeing), selecting the right input (understanding) and adding your input effectively to the story (delivering).

What we have provided in this part of the book is some of the repertoire or inputs that we have seen be effective and to give pointers as to when they can be best used. There is a risk that this approach will feel disjointed without the overall story. It is only when you bring these discrete activities together in real life that they create music.

Therefore don't think of yourself as a manager while reading, for now you are a jazz musician preparing for another steamy New Orleans night . . .

To get you in the mood, this is what one such jazz drummer told us about improvisation.

It's interesting that in jazz there are many pre-established rules, formats, and changes that many will use when improvising. Like improvised comedy, if you don't know these hidden forms it's downright impossible to leap in and 'improv with' a bunch of players. Typically there's a lot of interaction outside of the music, too – eye contact, a gesture, a grimace, a nod. These are important particularly when the players don't really know each other well . . .

When playing there's a level of activity that is pretty unconscious – you can chug out a rhythm without really thinking about it. So your mind is left to guide on a more general level – I'm not thinking about every touch, every note I'm hitting. I'm thinking more about the feel, the emotion, the centre of the musical story. The aim is to respond to what another person has laid out. Choosing exactly how to respond is very situational – it depends on what has happened before, where the song has come from, and where it might go from here.

Success comes from trusting the others, levels of patience, giving room to each other, knowing where each other is coming from. Knowing your 'voice' – how your instrument speaks with others, it's range of tone and dynamics, knowing how it can add (or subtract).

So perhaps it is not as easy to follow this simple process as it might first seem, but with practice it is very achievable. Let us preview each part of the process before attacking each in more detail.

Seeing

Increasing your ability to see and recognize what is really happening around you is about seeing your situation from different angles. This enables you to take new approaches, to get a new grip on your situation. The aim is to increase your sensitivity to the important factors, to develop the alertness required to direct and focus your attention.

We do this in this book in two ways. First, by encouraging you personally to view old problems in new ways. Throughout the book we look at the situations we have found from a few key angles. Spotted any yet?

Well, one is exactly what we are talking about here. The importance of recognizing what's going on in the territories through which you are travelling. This is where most ideas fall. They don't get into action, they get stuck in the gap between the idea and the action. The idea–action gap is a complex and political space, where you'll need your wits about you.

The idea–action gap is a complex and political space, where you'll need your wits about you.

Another angle? Making sense, and making use. A virtuous circle, a learning cycle, that should characterize your movement across the territory. Thoughtful action and active thinking. Not one or the other, but both.

A further angle is keeping things mindsized. Success comes in the moment, therefore only the memorable is useful. You won't get value out of something that you can't call to mind. The world of business is full of complicated models and ideas, more than we recall; what you want is a way of gaining instant access, when you need it. This comes through ideas, frameworks that fit your mind. Small ideas that make big differences. The mindsized.

There'll be more. Keep looking.

Our second way of focusing your attention is to point out key patterns that exist in this complexity, features of the terrain. Complex and dynamic it is, but chaotic it is not. There is shape, albeit of a higher order. We will be introducing a simple framework to clarify this shape. It can act as a lens to view the world, one that allows you to sort and prioritize the mass of information available to you as you manage your talent. More on that shortly.

Understanding

Understanding what you and your talented person want can only be achieved by dialogue. A key feature of managing talent, as we have already explained, is that it is a shared process. The quality of your relationship is central to achieving understanding. The greater the trust between you, the more each of you will be able to be open about your needs and wants.

We will look at some of the skills you will require to do this successfully. We focus on two of the most basic capabilities you need as a manager – your ability to think and to talk.

Delivering

It is all very well to know what you need to do, but you have to be able to deliver on it. Some of this will be straightforward. The 'stock in trade' of being a manager. Some of it isn't. Again, the quality of your thinking and your talking are fundamental to your ability to deliver effectively, to make things happen in the complex and political world that is typical of organizations today.

When it comes to managing talented people, we believe that the challenge of delivering has fundamental implications for the manager's role, and for the manager personally. If you haven't already read the second part of this book, *a theory on managing talent*, you will find our views on that issue there. In the present section the emphasis is on the more immediate practicalities of managing the interaction: *seeing, understanding and delivering*.

Our practical advice on managing day-to-day interactions with talented people revolves around this approach. It is not a rigid sequence of steps. Real life does not present its challenges neatly packaged like that. Our approach is not a ladder. It is more like a puzzle, where you may have to go through the pieces several times to explore how they fit together to arrive at a solution. At the same time, there is a broad sequence: seeing, understanding, delivering. Just as you start with the edge pieces in a jigsaw. But you should expect to go through several iterations with the pieces. It's a process of progressive problem-solving.

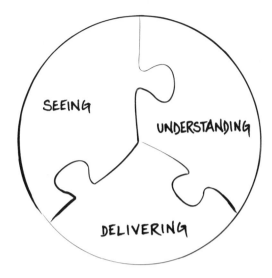

OK, let's begin by going back to the first piece of the puzzle and developing a clear picture of what is going on. To help you do this we want to introduce you, in the next section, to a way of spotting the patterns that underlie the issues of managing talent.

1 – seeing what is happening

Before you can act successfully, you need to unravel the complexity of what's going on. As we have said, we do not believe that complexity brings chaos. It may feel like that at times, but we believe that there is an underlying pattern that, once seen, can allow you to discern order in the apparent chaos. More specifically, it will provide a new lens through which to view the challenges of managing talent and assist you to manage them.

Before we turn to the particular challenges of managing talented people, let's establish a broader context about the challenges of managing.

This broader conceptual framework, the lens if you like, is not our invention. It was put forward, and compellingly argued, by Robert Keidel in his book, *Seeing Organisational Patterns* (Berrett-Koehler, 1995).

It will particularly appeal to you if you are tired of the two by two matrix as a way of representing management situations.

Keidel argues that management is essentially all about the difficulties of reconciling three divergent, but necessary requirements: the need for control, the need for autonomy and the need for co-operation. We call it the 'trilemma' of management.

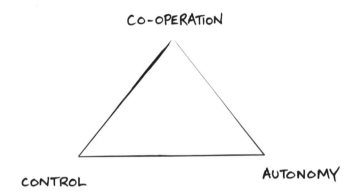

These are the three underlying requirements of effective organization, although they are more familiar in less abstract forms. Control is the need for decision-making. Co-operation is the need for teamworking. Autonomy is the need for individual action.

The trouble is that these requirements do not sit easily together, as we all know from our own experience. Decisiveness can bruise relationships within the team and with the individual who feels unheard. Team harmony can come at the cost of ignoring individual opinion and can involve a loss of momentum. Individual freedom of action can carry a price ticket in terms of the cohesiveness of the group or the quality of the decision reached. So, although control, co-operation and autonomy are all necessary, each creates tensions for the others.

Managers need to pay attention to them all. But, attending to one inevitably creates the risk of neglecting the others, and therefore of solving one problem at the expense of creating another. It's a balancing act. A continuous process, balancing and rebalancing on an ongoing basis. That's why management is so difficult.

You have to keep moving.

And this is where so much of the advice that is dispensed to managers can be positively unhelpful. The notion that you should develop a particular style. That there's such a thing as 'best practice.' That there is one, if not right, then at least preferable, way of doing things.

The trouble with that approach is that it tends to push you off balance. Ironic, isn't it? The more you try to develop a clear and solid approach, the harder you are likely to find it to maintain your balance. Being more fixed makes you less steady.

Now let's consider the challenge of managing talented people through this lens. The three basic issues involved in managing are control, co-operation and autonomy. Managers commonly make the mistake of giving too much attention to one of these issues at the expense of the others. Given these assumptions then it is easy to see four obvious, distinct styles that can be adopted when it comes to managing talented people.

Four?

Yes, four.

One at each extremity and one in the middle. We call it 'lurching around'. Not exactly a style, but certainly an observable pattern. It's what happens when you aren't clear about what's going on or, more importantly when you don't have much idea why. Then you shift from one emphasis to another as your attention becomes taken up with the latest problem.

One moment you're encouraging people to express their opinions freely, the next moment you're asserting your position as the manager and telling them what you've decided, the next you're arranging some social event to repair team spirit.

Lurching around. About as much style as a headless chicken.

And an approach that will inspire talent about as much as being led by one.

A CO-OPERATIVE STYLE:
INVOKING TEAMWORK
EMPHASIZING THE RELATIONSHIP

LURCHING AROUND

A CONTROLLING STYLE:
INVOKING AUTHORITY

AN EMPOWERING STYLE:
ALLOWING AUTONOMY

These approaches may be obvious, but are they effective?

The extreme styles actually represent two of the three ways to fail, according to Keidel.

Three ways to fail:

1 having no priorities;

2 overdoing your top priority;

3 underdoing your bottom priority.

Well 'lurching around' is clearly number 1 and dominant styles number 2. The third way to fail, number 3, is subtler. It sees the challenge of managing as a dichotomy. That is, as a trade off between two of the three requirements – autonomy and control or co-operation and autonomy and so on.

We've described the problem of having no priorities. Overdoing your top priority is also easily illustrated. Too much emphasis on autonomy allows people to become unaccountable or self-indulgent;

too much control and you will come across as a dictator; too much attention to co-operation and your leadership will feel hesitant and indecisive.

We can therefore map the area within the triangle where viable strategies exist.

The clear areas represent the viable strategies. The ones that achieve a balance between all three requirements.

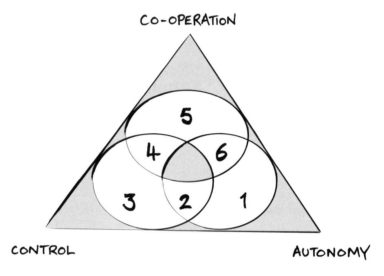

If you want to give names to these strategies, you might distinguish them like this:

1 freedom of expression with respect for others and a clear purpose;

2 negotiation, in the context of the team;

3 decision making with concern for individual views and consensus;

4 finding an agreed way forward;

5 team cohesion with scope for individual contributions to a shared purpose;

6 arriving at a consensus of opinion, recognizing a common goal.

OK, so that's fine. You need to adopt an approach that balances control, autonomy and co-operation. But how do you decide on the right combination for a particular set of circumstances? More specifically, how do you decide what balance is required when it comes to managing talented people?

To answer that question, we'll start by looking at the trilemma another way.

It requires us to take the analysis a level deeper. Because the blame can't simply be laid at the manager's door. (That makes a change, we hear you say.)

We've already established that there are inherent tensions to be managed in the relationship between manager and talent. The trilemma can be used to think about where these tensions come from. Essentially, it seems to us, there are three sources of tension: the manager, the talented person, and third parties. Consider each in turn.

How do managers tend to create tensions in the relationship?

◆ by holding on to the talent for too long;

◆ by exposing the talented person prematurely;

◆ by fostering dependence;

◆ by holding unrealistic or unclear expectations.

How do talented people tend to create tensions in the relationship?

◆ by overstepping the mark;

◆ by performing below expectations;

◆ by not making enough effort to develop relationships with others (being *too* personally resourceful);

◆ by being inconsistent.

How do third parties tend to create tensions in the relationship between managers and their talented people?

◆ by poaching that talent;

- by whinging about elitism or the manager's inconsistency towards them;
- by complaining about some aspect of the talent's behaviour;
- by 'blowing hot and cold' about the talent.

Seems complex at first sight. But what's the pattern below the surface of this complexity? Essentially simple. And another example of the different ways of failing to balance the trilemma. It is all too easy to give too much attention to one of the three fundamental issues at stake in management, while giving too little attention to the others. Each party can make this mistake.

For example, holding on to the talented person for too long is an extreme of control from the manager, without sufficient consideration of the talent's need for freedom of action (autonomy) or the quality of their relationship (co-operation). Exposing the talented person prematurely is a case of allowing too much autonomy and so on. Check the rest of the list.

So we might consider a 'system' of interrelated trilemmas.

We've been saying that managing talented people is a S.P.E.C.I.A.L. problem. This picture illustrates it. Shared, Political, Emergent, Complex, Individual, Active, Live! More importantly, this diagram shows where these characteristics come from. From the varying approaches that can be adopted, and the consequent tensions that arise, in any particular interaction by those involved.

Let's go back for a moment to the classic talent problems that we sketched at the beginning of this part of the book and see how they might be interpreted, using this lens.

At first sight, they seem to fall neatly into place.

The Ultimatum, for instance, where the talent exploits its value to force a bargain, looks like a case where the talented person is

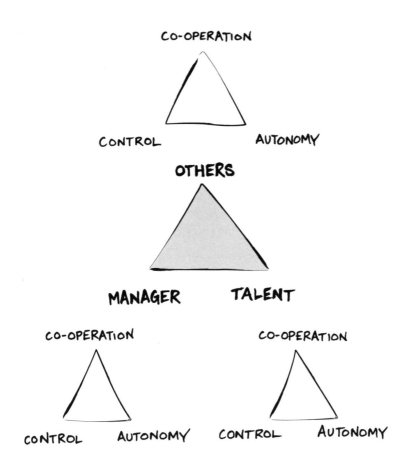

CO-OPERATION

CONTROL   AUTONOMY

OTHERS

MANAGER   **TALENT**

CO-OPERATION   CO-OPERATION

CONTROL   AUTONOMY   CONTROL   AUTONOMY

neglecting co-operation in an attempt to gain more control in its own interests, a negotiating strategy.

The Prima Donna, where the talent makes a particularly valuable contribution but consistently upsets others in the process, again looks like neglect of co-operation.

The Runaway Enthusiast, where talent overreaches its authority, looks like a case of extreme autonomy, disregarding the need for control.

The Poachers, where another manager seeks to lure your talent away, might be seen as others engaged in independent action (excessive autonomy) without sufficient consideration for the overall interests of the business (control) or their subsequent relationship with you (co-operation).

But these are superficial readings. Not wrong, but not as deep or useful as they might be. You'll notice that they each focus only on one party, the apparent prime mover in the situation. But they say nothing about the rest of the system, the other parties involved. The problem is shared and political, remember.

So, acknowledging the emergent quality of managing talented people, we will pause this analysis of classic cases, while we turn our attention to the next piece of the puzzle, understanding what each of you wants.

As we said, the process is one of progressive problem-solving.

2 – understanding what each of you wants

We have already said, and as a practising manager you will know, that the quality of a relationship has a major bearing on reaching an understanding.

What is required is a dynamic quality in the relationship between talent manager and talented person. It needs to be dynamic because that is the nature of management, expected to handle multiple demands, changing situations, continuous time pressure. It also needs to be dynamic because that is the nature of talent, urgent, impatient, keen to be on the move.

Achieving a dynamic quality in the relationship depends on reaching the *shared* understanding of the context in which they are working at that point in time, and of their respective expectations and roles. Therefore not only do each of you need to be personally effective, but you need to be jointly effective. You need to make sense of what is happening together.

Before we get to that we need to put in place some building blocks. The complex and interactive nature of the S.P.E.C.I.A.L. environment means that two capabilities – thinking and talking – are particularly critical. Frankly, you can't get much more basic than thinking and talking, they are a natural part of everyday life. And therein lies the problem. As processes they come too naturally, unconsciously often, so much so that they risk going unnoticed.

Until now.

Well actually until our previous book, *Clued Up: Working through Politics and Complexity* (momentum, 2002). But just in case you haven't had the pleasure, we will briefly revisit the main points here.

Firstly, thinking. The questions posed by the talented are often demanding, the answers often unobvious. By definition they make you think. So here is how to improve your thinking.

Good – a distinctive brand of thinking

The most basic shortcoming in human thinking is the tendency to fail to step it up a gear when necessary. Most of the time our thinking is automatic and can proceed largely unconsciously. Our 'default' setting, as David Perkins – a Harvard-based authority on the subject – puts it, is 'hasty, narrow, fuzzy and sprawling'. And that's usually OK when we're dealing with things that are familiar, where an approximation will suffice, when near enough is good enough, or when the risks associated with poor thinking are not high.

However . . .

Managing talented people is an area where the stakes are high. It is political, complex, dynamic. The sort of circumstances where default thinking is likely to get you into trouble. And fast.

'Good' is the antidote to default thinking. It is the approach to take in S.P.E.C.I.A.L. circumstances.

G is for give thinking time.
O is for open it.
O is for organize it.
D is for deepen it.

Give thinking time

Yes, we know time is scarce, especially for managers. We know you are under pressure to get things done. But here is the paradox. Giving time makes time. Giving time to thinking makes our subsequent actions more effective, by shaping our ideas and actions more appropriately.

Thinking is an integral part of action. Ignore it at your peril. Acting without thinking is simply reflex, or instinct. And risky.

In practical terms, the way to give time to thinking is very simple. It is by interrupting whatever else we are doing. We do this as a matter of course for people or events that we like or value. It's simply a case of doing the same for thinking. Especially when it comes to thinking about managing talented people. As one of our interviewees succinctly put it, *'Now that I come to think of it, we don't really give enough thought to this.'*

Giving time to thinking is a high leverage action. A little bit of time invested in thinking can yield a disproportionate return; even a few minutes of organized thinking action can make a big difference.

Open your thinking

The reason for giving time to thinking is to improve its quality and the first ingredient of quality thinking is for it to be open.

One of the hallmarks of good thinking is that it is open to possibilities. It does not leap to conclusions in situations where the evidence is unclear or the risks of a mistake are high. Good thinking is on the look out for alternative interpretations.

Good thinking is on the look out for alternative interpretations.

Being open in our thinking is not so much a question of technique as one of mindset. We don't actually need a toolkit of problem solving methods or have to remember an array of step-by-step procedures to be open in our thinking. We simply need to approach things in an open-minded way. It's a matter of disposition, taking a mindful approach.

To be mindful:

First, be open to new information. Take in new data without prejudging their significance or screening them out because they don't immediately seem to fit our expectations.

Second, be open to multiple perspectives rather than having only one frame of reference to guide your actions.

Third, continually create new categories, new classifications, actively looking for new and unobvious ways of making sense of information.

Organize your thinking

It's easier to use our thinking effectively, to direct it towards dealing with particular problems and challenges, if it is organized. How do we organize our thinking? Here are three ways of going about it.

In or out?

At the most general level, we have the choice of taking our thinking in one of only two directions: out or in. If our thinking seems to be stuck on one particular point or issue and simply going round in circles, then it's time to head outwards, time for some divergent thinking. So generate more options, explore more possibilities. If our thinking seems to be overwhelmed by too many ideas or too much data, then it's time to narrow it down. In that case we need to use convergent thinking, prioritizing, applying explicit criteria, rank ordering, and other focusing devices.

Step-wise

Another way of organizing our thinking is to design a process for it. Tools like the problem-solving wheel are essentially of this sort, step-by-step approaches to guide the application of our thinking and other forms of action. What is important is not to feel compelled to follow these tools slavishly.

Management is a practical world that's primarily interested in effective answers, so don't get hung up about 'right' answers or 'right' processes. Devise your own processes. A step-by-step process is only a strategy for dealing with a challenge. It's only valuable if it's useful. If it isn't useful, design one that is. One that moves things forward.

Frameworks as organizers

A third way of organizing our thinking is by applying a particular frame of reference and using that to provide structure and boundaries for our thinking.

Frames of reference can be established at many different levels, from the paradigm of the scientific approach, with its emphasis on objectively observed, replicable data, on economy of explanation and on the disproof of alternatives, to specific tools, like SWOT analysis (strengths, weaknesses, opportunities and threats).

Again, there is no right or wrong level for a frame of reference. It is a question of usefulness rather than correctness. Which organizer we choose is less important than the discipline of using one (or preferably more than one – to make our thinking open), so that we can get our thinking moving and follow the train of thought.

It is essential, when using any framework or model or concept as an organizer, to recognize what you're doing. You are coming at the issue from a particular angle. If you don't recognize that, then the organizer can easily become a trap that will ultimately constrain rather than improve your thinking.

So choose an organizer and get started.

Deepen your thinking

We can be liberal in our choice of organizer because organizing our thinking is not an end in itself, but a means to an end. The real goal is comprehension that we can use in practice. So good thinking requires depth of understanding.

How do we make our thinking deep?

What we mean by deep is sound or coherent. Deep thinking produces reliable explanations, ones that we can trust to predict how things will work.

But here's the difficulty. The world we live and work in is seldom as predictable as we would wish. So deep thinking starts to sound unrealistic, unattainable and therefore irrelevant for people who have to be pragmatic, people in business and management. But when understanding is at a premium, as it is in managing talent, then deep thinking is not a luxury but a necessity. We need to understand how things are happening and why. We need to make sense of the dynamics of what's going on. Because if we don't, the only certainty is that we will find ourselves left behind by events.

Unfortunately a particular weakness in human thinking, particularly when we are under pressure, is to think in terms of oversimplistic patterns of cause and effect. We tend to overlook the possibility of multiple causes and multiple effects. We don't think ahead to the second and third-order repercussions. We tend to see the obvious and stop at that, rather than seeking out the less obvious, but more powerful explanations.

What can we do to remedy this? For a start, resist the temptation to seize on the first, or obvious, explanation. It might be the best we can come up with, but before we decide we should think-test it out. Make yourself think of at least one alternative explanation?

Secondly, compare and contrast your explanations. This helps to expose the assumptions and the logic – or the lack of it – behind them. It makes your thinking deeper by making it more careful.

Thirdly, expose your explanation to scrutiny. Try your explanation out on someone else, or ideally a number of other people, but do it individually so that you get the full value of their independent views. This will oblige you to express your explanation clearly. It's a good clue that your thinking isn't deep enough, if other people can't make sense of what you're trying to say.

Finally, stay open to other possible explanations. Pay attention, as events unfold – that 'emergent' phenomenon – to information which might cause you to revise and refine your original explanation.

So, that is an outline of what we mean by Good thinking. It is not a rigid procedure, not a sequence of steps to be followed. Again, it is more in the nature of an approach, a set of mindful dispositions to be drawn upon, flexibly, as we work our way through a thinking challenge.

To be technical for a moment, Good thinking is about heuristics rather than algorithms. Whereas an algorithm is a series of prescribed steps that are guaranteed to lead to the required answer, heuristics are like rules of thumb. They will take you in the right direction, improve the odds, but won't in themselves guarantee a right answer.

Which is as good as it gets, because none of us live or work in a world of certainties, either managing in general, or managing talent in particular. Managing is a practical business in a probabilistic world.

Good thinking – together

We have explained the relevance of good thinking in general terms and you will probably already have recognised how it can assist with seeing what's happening, the first element of our three part approach to managing talent in practice. Now let us connect it more specifically to the central theme of this section, the task of understanding what each of you wants.

The short answer is by doing good thinking together. How do you do that? You won't be surprised by our answer.

Give time for thinking together. Make time for each other. Because talented people are more than averagely capable, it's easy to fall into the trap of leaving them to get on with things. To give them less time than others. But that's a recipe for drifting apart, for undermining the quality of the relationship. So make time to do thinking together. A good way to use talent is to involve them in some of the broader issues that require your attention. That will make them feel valued and involved and simultaneously give you the opportunity to stay close and to understand how their thinking is developing. This is important because, as we have seen, talented people develop quickly. You need to make time to stay in touch.

A good way to use talent is to involve them in some of the broader issues that require your attention.

Open your thinking together. Invite talent's views and perspectives. Set out your own, side by side, as alternative perspectives. Don't fall into the mistake of critiquing views prematurely, of setting up a combative, either-or dialogue. Model open-mindedness and the exploration of ideas. In a relationship where you are confident that your opinions will be listened to, non-judgementally, and heard, you are far more likely to reveal what's really on your mind. This will enable you to create new possibilities together, possibilities that you are both prepared to explore.

Organize your thinking together. One of the particular contributions that you can make as a manager of talent is to model good thinking, to show your people not only its importance but also how to achieve it in practice. Conspicuous organization of your thinking is a good way of going about doing this. And the explicit use of an organizer, for instance, is an obvious starting point. That is one reason why we have provided a number of relevant organizers in this book.

Deepen your thinking together. As we said above, you don't use organizers for their own sake but as a means towards an end. The objective is understanding. In managing talented people, where misaligned expectations are so often at the root of the problems encountered, deep thinking is crucial to enable you to see what is happening and to understand what each of you wants. Deep thinking reveals the dynamics of your interactions. Managing talent is a dynamic process. You are both active participants in the process.

You need to be equally active participants in the process of making sense of the proceedings.

Don't keep the principles of good thinking to yourself. Share them with your talent. Not only will this make them more personally effective, it will also make your interactions more productive and, vitally, it will reduce the prospect of misunderstanding. If you both employ the principles of good thinking, then you will be doubly alert to default thinking. (Two tracking stations will pick up more signals than one!) Your thinking, and your commitment to that thinking, will be shared in a way that it is otherwise unlikely to be.

Quite apart from anything else, good thinking feels good. And the quality of a relationship is a lot to do with how it feels.

Back to the classics

In the last chapter we introduced the trilemma organizer and suggested that it was a powerful lens for managers of talent to get an insightful picture of what was going on. We also started to re-examine some of the classic problems of managing talented people through this lens. Now we'd like to extend that analysis, applying the principles of good thinking to make it even more useful.

Without good thinking it is easy to default into seeing these classic situations narrowly and shallowly. Seeing the Ultimatum as being held to ransom by the unco-operative talent, the Prima Donna as the self-centred talent, the Poacher as the self-interested third party and so on. Essentially stereotypes. Default thinking. Dangerous thinking.

Give the thinking some more time, open it up, organize it – by using the broader system of trilemmas – and look for deeper explanations. What happens?

For a start it takes us beyond one dimensional thinking. In the case of the Ultimatum, we need to think not just about what the talent is doing but also about the other people involved. Suppose we add only one other perspective. What does the manager want in this situation? Well, the short answer is that we don't know. But the trilemma reminds us that there is a range of possibilities. She might want to exert control. This might entail resisting the talent's challenge, or equally trying to find a solution but only within particular constraints. Alternatively, she might opt for a co-operative response. This might mean simply giving in to talent's demand, or alternatively appealing to the talent not to endanger relationships by 'rocking the boat' or equally it might mean appealing to her relationship with her own boss to find an acceptable solution. Yet again, she could respond in an autonomous mode. This might mean taking a purely self-centred view, refusing to do anything that might put herself at risk, or equally it might take the form of sympathizing with the talent's demand and encouraging him/her to pursue it.

Hmm . . . And we haven't even considered where third parties might be coming from, although that is likely to be highly relevant, and not only in this case.

Nor have we yet considered the deeper thinking, into the dynamics of the situation, how it might unfold, what might emerge, what the talent might do next or how the manager could respond to that next move, and so on.

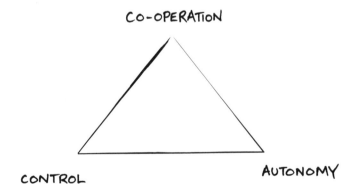

The point we are making is this: the 'classic' talent problems look familiar, but you do not need to apply much good thinking to any of them to recognize that an initial reading does not reveal much about what might actually be going on. Or, to put it another way, even a small investment in good thinking will lead to a more open-minded, less precipitate and less risky assessment of what is happening and of the actions that you might then take. All of which will help to improve the quality of your relationship with your talent and your ability to align expectations and to resolve issues with them.

We believe this example should be sufficient to make the point. If you are still unconvinced and want to work through some of the other classic cases, now would be a good time to do so. We think you may find the most compelling evidence in what is one of the most common talent problem scenarios, the Fallen Star. This is the situation where talent encounters a setback, fails to live up to their anticipated potential or to deliver against expectations.

What is the explanation for the Fallen Star? And, more importantly, what's to be done? Can you generalize answers to these two questions? In our view, the answer to that final question is an emphatic No! In S.P.E.C.I.A.L. circumstances, like managing talented people, generalizations don't work. And yet we have often witnessed a hasty, narrow, shallow, default answer in practice. The star falls and people shrug and say, *'I guess he wasn't as talented as we thought after all.'*

Have you ever seen that happen? It is hardly a demonstration of understanding. But it is also a timely reminder that seeing what is happening and understanding what each of you wants are not sufficient. You still have to deliver in practice. So we will turn to that issue in the next chapter.

3 – delivering skilfully

If good thinking is the antidote to complexity, then talking provides the key to interactivity. The quality of conversation you have with your talent is critical. Like thinking, dialogue is often such an automatic part of life that we don't notice the patterns that exist. And because we don't pay it much close attention, we use it less deliberately than we might. Less deliberately than we ought, if we want to use it to good effect. So this chapter offers some help in recognising conversational patterns, so that you can use dialogue effectively to resolve the issues of managing talented people.

Conversational patterns

The management of a conversation, by definition, is shared, or more accurately negotiated, between those taking part. Direction, pace, content and style are, to a greater or lesser extent, being contested from moment to moment, in the moment, throughout any conversation that we have. No wonder it can be difficult to use talking to do what we want.

Conversation is, like the nature of managing talented people, S.P.E.C.I.A.L. Shared, Political, Emergent, Complex, Individual,

Active and Live! It's no coincidence. That is why conversation is the means for delivering results in this area. It is the only means matched to the nature and demands of the challenge.

The implication is that we have to be skilful in managing conversation. But the difficulty is, as we have just seen, that you cannot unilaterally control a conversation, any more than you can unilaterally control a talented person. The process is co-created, whether you like it or not. Yet while you cannot expect to control a dialogue, you can aim to take the lead in ensuring that it is co-created. And you should. That is part of your responsibility as a manager and where your skills and approach can improve the probability of delivering a mutually satisfactory outcome.

Preparation is part of the answer, but can only be part of it. We can prepare for the start of our conversations (although people don't do that as often as they should). We can think carefully beforehand about what we want to say, how we want to say it, what sort of different reactions we might get, and how we might respond to each of those possibilities. But we can't anticipate or rehearse everything. We have quite a lot of control over the launch of the proceedings, but after that the system we call conversation very rapidly becomes much more dynamic, complex and difficult to steer.

How can we manage this process of co-creation in the moment?

Once again, having an organizer helps. It won't provide a guarantee, but it will improve the odds. It gives us a map that can help us to keep track of where the conversation is, moment to moment. So let's build this organizer.

As with other maps, you start by figuring out where you are now before deciding where you want to go next. And you do the first of those things by positioning yourself in relation to the questions that you need to be answering before you can expect to deliver successfully: do I see and understand what's going on? Have I spotted all the clues? Am I clued up?

If we feel clear about things, sure of what is going on, then we can simply go ahead and act. On the other hand, if we feel unsure, then we need to investigate first. But, as we've seen, you can't act in isolation in a conversation. You have to think about other people's views and interests, especially talented people. They will be attempting to influence your views and you will need to influence theirs. So there's another dimension in the conversational territory that needs to be considered: whether you agree or disagree with what the other person is saying.

In practice, of course, we usually have to deal with both dimensions at the same time, so in effect the territory for any conversation looks like this.

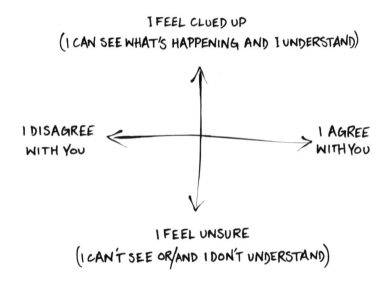

I FEEL CLUED UP
(I CAN SEE WHAT'S HAPPENING AND I UNDERSTAND)

I DISAGREE WITH YOU

I AGREE WITH YOU

I FEEL UNSURE
(I CAN'T SEE OR/AND I DON'T UNDERSTAND)

Think about this conversational territory for a minute. Some parts of it offer a firm basis for a dialogue. Others don't.

It does not make sense for me to decide whether I agree or disagree with you, unless I'm feeling sure about what's going on. The further away we are from being sure about what's going on, the further away we should be from committing ourselves to either agreeing or disagreeing.

Therefore there are parts of this territory that are relatively safe, easier to negotiate than others. Other parts are crazy space! Agreeing, or even disagreeing, with someone when we have no idea what is going on (and we've never done that, have we?). Other parts are risky, but viable. You are only on solid ground when you are clued up. This is when you can confidently make choices. The safer places are marked by the triangle on our map.

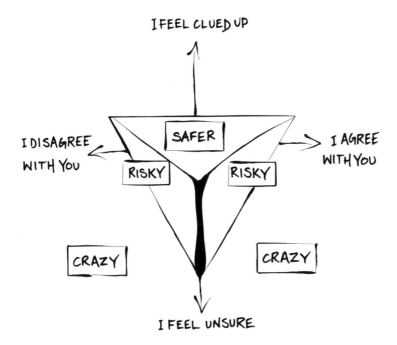

One of the advantages of this little framing device is that it's very easy to use. Essentially we only have to ask ourselves two questions to get a sense of where we are:

1 How sure do I feel about what's going on?

2 Do I agree with what you're saying?

These do the job, because you don't need exact answers; you need ready ones. Reasonable estimates that you can make easily in the moment, in the stream of conversation.

Now, before we go on, let's just illustrate this idea of conversational territory with an example. Here's a small, but non-trivial instance from our own experience of when a manager failed to map the territory of an important conversation with a talent.

Here's a small, but non-trivial instance from our own experience of when a manager failed to map the territory of an important conversation with a talent.

Towards the end of a performance review discussion the talented person initiated a new line of discussion with the words, *'I've been thinking about my career.'* To which the manager quickly responded, bringing the dialogue to an abrupt halt, *'Don't you worry about that. We'll see that you're all right.'* Nothing further was said, but the talent went away furious at the condescending way in which he had been treated, when what he had been looking for was a joint exploration of possibilities, while the manager went away believing he had just carried out an effective act of retention!

Was the manager clued up before acting? No. Was his conversational move a good one? Hardly. Did he think through the alternatives open to him before acting? It doesn't look like it.

Conversational moves

Conversation is dynamic. It's a series of moves. So what moves can we make? What options are available? Listening to the ebb and flow of conversation, in all its natural untidiness, it sounds as if there might be an infinite number of moves. But essentially there are only three. A move towards each of the points of the conversational range. A move to take you towards each of the three cardinal points of the conversational territory. We've named these moves to reflect their purpose. We call them the Counter, the Reinforce and the Probe.

We've named these moves to reflect their purpose. We call them the Counter, the Reinforce and the Probe.

The Counter is an expression of disagreement. It may be defensive, in response to what someone else has said, or it may be more pre-emptive, stating your position. Either way, the move is essentially a blocker. It is designed to force the interaction either towards or away from a particular direction. What does it sound like? *'No.' 'I disagree.' 'I don't accept that.' 'What I want is . . .' 'You're wrong.' 'I'm right and here's why.' 'Don't you worry about that.'*

The Reinforce is an expression of agreement. Again, you may use it either as a response, an expression of support, or more proactively, perhaps as an exhortation or a reminder. Either way, the function of this move is to be an accelerator. It is designed to nudge the interaction in a certain direction. What does it sound like? *'Yes.' 'I agree.' 'Also we could . . .' 'I think you're absolutely right.' 'What I'd like to add to that is . . .' 'We'll see that you're all right.'*

You'll have noticed that the common factor behind both these moves is that in each case we're reasonably sure about things, about what we want, about where the other person is coming from and so on. And when we are sure, these are very appropriate moves. However, too often our conversations are not based on a solid foundation of understanding. That's why we've drawn the conversational triangle balanced precariously on its tip rather than resting safely on a broad foundation. And that's why the Probe move is so important. It builds the foundations without which the Counter and the Reinforce moves can so often produce unintended, and undesirable, effects.

So what is the Probe? It's an expression of enquiry. It is a means to reduce uncertainty, to open things up, explore them, resolve puzzles and establish understanding, in other words, create a basis for deciding what directions are viable. It is the conversational move that is too often missing. What does it sound like? *'What exactly are you saying?' 'I'm not clear. Can you tell me more?' 'Another way of looking at that might be . . .' 'Let's consider some alternatives.' 'What would be the implications of that?' 'What are the various advantages and disadvantages?'*

The Probe is the move that the manager in our example above needed to make. Did he know what the talent was saying? No, he simply leapt to a conclusion, made a pre-emptive strike, the Counter to limit further discussion followed instantly by a quick Reinforce to try to maintain the relationship. Wrong moves! Bad result.

The Probe is the move that the manager in our example above needed to make.

If we are to manage dialogue successfully, we need to have and to use the whole repertoire of moves, and we need to choose our moves carefully. Because conversation takes place, by definition, out in the open. There's not much cover if you make a mistake. You need a simple, mind-sized organizer like this one, because the stakes can be high; it's all happening in real time and someone else is involved.

That is part of the value of this organizer. It helps you to recognize quickly what moves the other person is making. Which, in turn, helps you to decide yours. Back to our example for a moment. What move did the talented person make? *'I've been thinking about my career.'* It's a Probe. It may not be expressed as a question, but it is clearly an invitation to open a dialogue on a topic. The smart move for the manager to have made would have been to Probe too. *'What have you been thinking?'* or *'What sort of conversation would you like us to have about that?'*

Take one more close look at the conversational territory and the range of conversational moves.

Notice the shape of the range of moves, the triangle that represents our viable scope for action. If we feel sure about what's going on, we've got some freedom to manoeuvre. We can agree or disagree, or have some qualified or conditional level of agreement somewhere in between. But when we're unsure about what's going on, then we're confined. The range of effective behaviours is much narrower. The

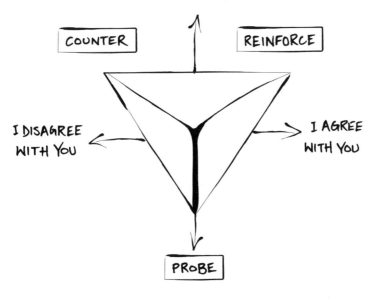

I FEEL CLUEDUP

COUNTER   REINFORCE

I DISAGREE   I AGREE
WITH YOU   WITH YOU

PROBE

I FEEL UNSURE

only safe move is to Probe, to enquire in order to gain
understanding. In other words, to make another iteration through
the process that remains the core of our practical advice for
managing talented people.

1   See clearly what is happening.

2   Understand what each of you want.

3   Deliver on it skilfully.

Alignment – working together

We've provided a picture of the territory in which conversations take
place, a way of knowing where you are and moving around the
space. A ready reckoner to carry in your head, a mental map. But
how do you use it to have effective conversations?

Well, think of how many times conversations appear to 'go wrong' or seem more difficult than they should, even when you are in fact both in agreement over the content. A common cause, from our observations, is a mismatch in type of conversation. Watch a conversation: one person probes, the other counters and already the wires are crossed.

We've seen it already in the little vignette we gave above.

The key to successful dialogue is alignment. Having your conversational map overlay with the other person's. That way you simplify the dynamics of the conversation and make your moves together, probing, countering and reinforcing in a co-ordinated dance. This allows both of you to pay attention to the content of the conversation rather than be confused by apparently inappropriate moves by your partner.

Alignment is another way of suggesting that you find your way *together* to the same part of the map. In other words, you take the trouble to ensure that you both have comparable certainty about what is going on and know the extent to which you agree or disagree. It is only at this point that you can address the substance of the conversation effectively, without being side-tracked by the moves that are being made.

In practical terms this means most conversations should start with both of you probing, asking questions. Even if you think you are sure, you need to be certain your discussion partner is as sure of their view. Without both of you being sure, one of you will end up in the crazy space – arguing from a very shaky position. Sounds obvious, but just watch how often conversations are led by bold statements of position rather than probing, data-gathering questions. And watch also how often dialogue disintegrates once one person is arguing from the crazy space.

In practical terms this means most conversations should start with both of you probing, asking questions.

Whether you move from Probing into Counter or Reinforce will depend on the content of your discussion. Either route is valid. Reinforcing and Countering are legitimate moves. You will need to use them to express your agreement and your disagreement. But you can't sensibly agree or disagree with each other in the absence of *shared* understanding. That is why the Probe is such a valuable, and needs to be such a recurring, move in conversation. Alignment relies on *maintaining* shared understanding.

Alignment relies on *maintaining* shared understanding.

As a manager you need to pay attention to that. Because without alignment you will set up conversational tensions and increase the risk that the dialogue will break down.

Some of the tensions are obvious. When you make a reinforcing move only to be met by a counter, for example. That will feel odd. Or when you are both countering. That will feel tense. Arguments do. So note that alignment is not about making the same move. It is about making complementary moves, moves which take the dialogue forward through the process of seeing what's going on, understanding what each other wants and enabling the delivery of a joint agreement, a mutually acceptable outcome, if one is possible.

It's our approach in action.

But don't underestimate the tensions that make this process difficult when you're trying to work together. These tensions are real, and they also have a familiar shape to them, as you may have noticed.

Probe and counter, reinforce and probe, counter and reinforce. Sound familiar? Earlier in the book we examined the underlying tensions for managers in general, and for the managers of talent in particular, between control, co-operation and autonomy. We shouldn't be surprised to find that underlying pattern emerging in conversations. A series of counters is a battle for control, reinforcements are a form of co-operation and when you are probing you do so from your own, autonomous position.

This is the nature of the territory.

So we'd like to offer you one more map. It's a development of the one we gave you earlier. Because – to return to the question at the start of this section – how you use these organizers to have effective conversations is by mapping how the conversation is going and making your moves accordingly. And you have to watch a conversation as an interaction. If you simply pay attention to your thoughts and your own moves, you won't be managing the conversation. It's a co-created process, remember.

This slightly more detailed map acknowledges that. It recognizes that there are two parties to the conversation. It's a fuller way of monitoring what's going on and intervening to lead the discussion in useful directions.

It's a matrix! (No management text would be complete without one.) It needs to be, because we're looking at an interaction. You'll see that we have simply plotted the three conversational moves along each axis. The moves that each of you can make. The cells then represent how the discussion is likely to feel, depending on where each of you are heading, and – more importantly – where you might reasonably go from there.

For greater clarity the matrix is built up in two stages, starting with the more extreme positions . . .

You read this map by first recognizing what conversational move you are making – reinforcing, probing or countering. And the other's move. Then look at what's happening when these moves meet.

You are reinforcing.	You are probing.	You are countering.	
Feels as if you're in agreement. May be worth one final probe to make sure you're not simply avoiding a difficult conversation.		Feels as if they are satisfied but you still have an unresolved issue. Encourage them to probe to understand it.	**The other person is reinforcing.**
	Both working to understand each other. Keep the probing going till you both feel clear enough to agree (reinforce) or disagree (counter).		**The other person is probing.**
Feels as if you're satisfied but they still have an unresolved issue. Probe to understand it.		Could feel uncomfortable, but may be necessary. If you get stuck in your corners, then you may have reached an impasse, but probe to check. It might reveal other possibilities.	**The other person is countering.**
You are reinforcing.	**You are probing.**	**You are countering.**	

And now the less obvious positions . . .

	They seem to be agreeing with you, so why are you still probing? If you're clear, reinforce or counter. If you're unclear, explain why you need to keep probing.		**The other person is reinforcing.**
You seem to be agreeing with them, so why are they still probing? Check it out.	*Both working to understand each other. Keep the probing going till you both feel clear enough to agree (reinforce) or disagree (counter).*	Feels as if they've hit a sticking point for you. Be careful not to get drawn into a counter-counter interaction. Better to explain through probing.	**The other person is probing.**
	Feels as if you've hit a point of disagreement for them. Keep probing to understand it.		**The other person is countering.**
You are reinforcing.	**You are probing.**	**You are countering.**	

You will notice that jointly probing is central, to the map, to conversational skill, to achieving alignment and to delivering successfully when it comes to working with talented people.

This is because the business of managing talented people, the action, takes place in discussions. It takes place in meetings with people, not only one-to-one with the talented person, but with significant others, talent management forums, your own boss, others whose behaviour can affect the use – or misuse – of talent in your organization. In each of these interactions your conversational skill will be critical to managing the process of aligning the respective expectations of those concerned.

You will be far more influential if you are conversationally skilful. It is at the heart of being able to carry out our practical advice for managing talented people.

1 See clearly what is happening.

2 Know what each of you want.

3 Deliver on it skilfully.

And at the end of the day, if in doubt – probe!

The approach in action

So what does it all look like in action? We will wrap up this part of the book by illustrating our recommended approach with a conversational cameo.

Imagine, if you will, (we're sure you can!) a nightmare day for the manager of talent. A day on which the manager is confronted with multiple challenges. As you read it, you might like to think about what points of the managerial trilemma the various participants are coming from. Also, spot the types of conversational moves that are being made by the different players, and the effects of these moves.

Our little drama unfolds over three scenes. It opens, in everyday fashion, with our manager, M (that can be either male or female, just like in the James Bond films!) about to go to a meeting, when s/he is interrupted by the sudden entrance of a member of staff, the talented TP.

Scene 1: M's Office

TP Hi. Look, I'm really sorry, but I've come to give you my resignation.

M What? Oh no!

TP Yes. I'm sorry. Here's my letter of resignation.

M [*Wants to say: Don't do this to me! But has the presence of mind to say instead . . .*] I'd like us to talk about this first.

TP There's really nothing to talk about, I'm afraid. I've been offered another job. It looks good and I've said I'll give it a go. I've already told them that I'll accept.

M [*Wants to say: Why didn't you come and talk to me first! But recognizes that this will sound like a criticism and instead says . . .*] I'd still like to understand what's attracting you to it.

TP Well, yes, I can tell you that, but I don't want you to try to talk me out of it. It's been a big decision.

M [*Thinking: You can say that again! You're the most talented person in my department, but actually says . . .*] I'm sure it has. You do know you're highly regarded by a lot of people here?

TP By some of them, I guess.

M Look, I really want us to have this conversation, but I was just off to a management meeting when you came in. Can we . . .

TP Sorry I interrupted. But you need to understand I've already said yes to their offer.

M I understand what you're saying there. What I'd like to find out is more about why. Can we meet this afternoon? I'll clear time in my diary.

TP OK. It'll have to be after 3.30. I've got other commitments till then.

M Fine. [*Thinking: anything but fine!*]

Scene 2: the management meeting

M   Before we get into the agenda, I'd just like to let you know that TP has told me that he has been offered another job.

Ma That's a pity.

Mb Good riddance, I say.

Mc I think TP's a bit flakey.

Md Who's TP?

M to Mb *[Resisting the temptation to draw unfavourable comparisons with some of the people in Mb's department]* What makes you say 'good riddance'?

Mb Everybody knows he's arrogant.

M *[Resisting the further temptation to suggest that it might take one to know one]* What does he do that makes you think that?

Mb He can be difficult. Everybody knows that.

M I hear what you think, but I still don't understand why. Can you give me an example of when?

Mb Sure. There was that time he overstepped his authority and committed us to that new software package.

M Yes, and it turned out to be a very good choice, as I recall.

Mb But he upset the IT Standards Committee in the process. They'd already decided to buy something else.

M But they endorsed his choice after the event. He was simply more in touch then they were, more aware about the problems that other organizations had been having with the stuff the Committee wanted to use.

Mb Well, I know some people felt he was just doing his own thing at the time. And for my part, I don't think it's good for either teamwork or discipline, if you let people ignore collective decisions.

Md Perhaps. But it sounds as if he's someone who's prepared to act on his beliefs. Is he also prepared to accept the responsibility when he gets it wrong?

M Yes. He's not afraid of accepting responsibility and if he misjudges something, then he makes a point of learning from it. Would you like me to give you some examples?

Md to Mc I'd like to hear why you think he's flakey first.

M And I'd like to understand what you mean by 'flakey'.

Mc Flakey, you know . . . not a safe bet; he might not have what it takes.

M Say more.

Mc I just think his reputation is running ahead of what he's actually delivered.

M I still don't get the point you're making, I'm afraid.

Mc OK, his name is always coming up, I accept that. Lots of people say he's good, technically sharp, full of new ideas and certainly eager. I saw these things when he helped on some project work with my people, but I don't know if he can manage people. That story we heard a few moments ago suggests he might not have the skills for that.

M He doesn't have much experience of being responsible for others yet. He hasn't mentioned it, but I could imagine it's something he wants to get.

Mc He certainly needs to produce some evidence that he can do it before I'd have him on my team. You can't just trust to someone's potential, whatever that means; you've got to go on how they actually perform.

M How do we think our people are going to acquire skills and experience, if we don't provide opportunities for them to do that?

Mc That's a good question. I guess we have to think about how much risk we're prepared to take.

Md Or what we risk if we don't take any. This guy sounds interesting. Have we lost him? Is the situation irretrievable?

M I don't know yet. I'm seeing him this afternoon. I'll let you know after that, because I might need some help.

Scene 3 – M's office, the same afternoon

M OK, so we're both clear – this is a conversation to enable me to understand what's going on to make you decide to bring me your resignation.

TP Yes, but . . .

M You don't want me to try to talk you out of it?

TP That's right.

M Well, help me understand your thinking.

TP It's just a great opportunity.

M In what ways?

TP To do some new stuff, learn some new tricks, move things along, you know.

M Did you feel that you wouldn't be able to do that here?

TP Yes . . . no . . . well, I don't know really. It's been great, but it's kind of slowed down recently. I think I've got into a bit of a rut.

M And you're satisfied that won't happen in the new place?

TP Don't know. I don't think so. Not for a while anyway.

M I'm still not clear about what exactly it is that's attracting you strongly enough to move away from what you've got here to go through the whole business of starting again. What's the difference?

TP Well there's more money for a start!

M I guessed there might be. Is it the same job?

TP No, that's the point really. It's a bigger job.

M So you'd expect there to be more money for it?

TP Yes. And the bit I'm really excited about is having to lead a group of people for the first time, not just informally like I've done here, when I've been on project teams, but formally in a manager's role. Did I not tell you that was something I was starting to get interested in? . . .

We're going to break off here. We're not going to give you a Hollywood ending. As we've said throughout, you have to co-create your own endings. These are imaginary conversations (although they resemble many that we have heard over the years), but they are not a fantasy. We're not saying this approach guarantees that the manager will turn the situation round, will persuade TP to withdraw his resignation, will influence other managers to make a people-management opportunity available. What we are saying is that the approach illustrated here will dramatically improve the odds of achieving these things.

What we are saying is that the approach illustrated here will dramatically improve the odds of achieving these things.

What is clear, we believe, is that this approach keeps possibilities open. It enables the business of managing talented people, the process of aligning and re-aligning expectations, individual and organizational, to continue in a way that simply does not happen once positions become fixed.

Pivotal moments in these cameo conversations occur when the participants show some willingness to adapt their thinking, to keep moving.

And you will have noticed that the conversational move that contributes the most to this approach is the probe, the skilful use of questioning. It's not the only move you need, but it is the small thing that makes the big difference. This is no accident. It is because the Probe is the principal ally of Good thinking. And Good thinking is the other skill that we have already described as essential for the practice of managing talented people. The Probe is the conversational move that fosters Good thinking because it gives time for thinking, opens thinking up, goes at least some way towards organizing it (especially if the thinking behind the probe is explained) and deepens understanding.

Good thinking and active talking. Basics, perhaps. But keys to performing effectively in highly dynamic, complex circumstances where individual issues are paramount, where the stakes are high, reaction time is limited, and the ability to create room to manoeuvre is vital. The challenges you face in managing talented people.

In closing this part of the book . . .

We have covered a lot of ground here. Our aim has been twofold – firstly to build your managerial repertoire, increasing your options for action and, secondly, to help you with your timing, developing a sense of when to use your new skills.

There is so much improvisation required with talented people that the practice of managing them is like being that jazz musician. Some ideas and frameworks here will help keep track of the vibe, the story line – the trilemma for example. Others give you practical steps to take, be it good thinking or active talking. Above all, though, only you can make music with them, which requires preparation, practice and application – support for which is the subject of the final part of the book . . .

managing talent in action

This brings us to the part that matters most, the actual experience
of managing talented people. This is where the content becomes
yours rather than ours. But because management life is hectic and
crowded, fast-paced and filled with competing demands, it isn't
easy either to make sense of what is going on or to make use of
what we have. Nor is it easy to consult a book while you're in the
thick of the action. But it needs work, both to draw the lessons out
of your past experience and to decide what to do to take an
existing situation forward. So we've put our support, another case
study and a couple of organizers, where they will be easier for you
to get at when you need them, through your computer on the
website, *www.business-minds.com*

You are likely to find what we have left here in the book particularly
useful if you are currently in the middle of figuring out how to
handle the challenge of a talented person and you'd like some
questions to start to organize your thinking.

a plan of action

Now let's help you to shape the present and the future. It's time for a 'p of a'. Time to put the ideas in this book to work for you (and your talent) in your own situation, now and going forward. In this section we provide an organizer for that purpose.

To help you we have summarized the sorts of questions we think you should be answering as you work through your situation. They are not intended as a prescriptive set, more as a way of provoking and shaping your thinking. There are no prizes for completion in itself. Choose to address the questions that seem most relevant to your situation. By the same token, if you avoid the difficult ones, you'll only be cheating yourself. This is a chance to give thinking time, before your talent forces the pace, as they are so inclined to do.

To help you we have summarized the sorts of questions we think you should be answering as you work through your situation. They are not intended as a prescriptive set, more as a way of provoking and shaping your thinking.

So this is where we hand over to you.

As this is preparation or planning, it does not slavishly follow the structure of our three part process described in the previous part, *the practice of managing talented people*. You may see themes in the questions that you recognize from that and other parts of this book. Our picture is that these questions should form the basis of a work-in-progress, one that you return to as you think and talk your way through the process, filling in missing data, reviewing the progress you have made, figuring out what remains to be resolved.

Managing talented people is tricky territory. There are no guaranteed steps to success. You need to go on surveying your situation, to consider different angles as you make sense of the issue, to make mindful decisions as you choose your next moves. We've clustered the questions North, South, East, West and Line of March. This is no more than a metaphor to remind you that it pays to look around broadly before deciding on the direction that you're going to take.

Enough preamble. Over to you . . .

North – underlying expectations

◆ What are your goals?

◆ What influence does the talented person have on these?

◆ What are their goals, both immediate and longer term?

◆ How would you describe your values?

◆ How would you describe their values?

◆ How sure are you of your talent's expectations?

◆ What evidence do you have?

◆ If you wanted to verify these expectations, what questions would you ask?

South – the issue

◆ What is the current issue you face with your talented person?

◆ How has he/she described it to you?

◆ What are other, neutral (or not so neutral) parties saying about it?

◆ What is your *ideal* outcome?

◆ How does it differ from his/her desired outcome?

◆ How would your talented person probably react to this?

◆ If you couldn't have your ideal outcome, what other result would be acceptable?

◆ What are the consequences of not resolving this issue?

◆ What probing questions would you ask to find out more?

East – the people

◆ How would you describe your relationship with your talented person?

◆ What does he/she think of you?

◆ What key events have shaped your relationship?

◆ How could the present issue impact on your relationship?

◆ List everyone with an interest in the outcome of the issue.

◆ What are their respective interests?

West – the dynamics of the situation

◆ What forces are helping to resolve the issue?

◆ What forces are preventing the issue from being resolved?

◆ How do these forces interact? What dynamics, patterns and relationships emerge as you think about them?

◆ What choices do you have? (Consider at least three.)

◆ How do you assess the consequences of each choice? (Think ahead.)

◆ How do you picture the situation? (What does it look like if you draw it?)

◆ Summarize in a paragraph the territory in which you are working, the context in which you have to deliver an outcome.

A line of march – the first steps

◆ Where are you puzzled or least confident? Where do you need to probe to be more confident?

◆ What are the most important things to achieve in moving towards a resolution of the issue?

◆ What has to be done right now?

◆ How could you take these actions while keeping as many future options open as you can?

◆ What actions can you (or/and your talented person) take to increase others' willingness to assist in resolving the issue?

◆ Who will you speak to and what will you actually say? (Your opening lines.)

And then . . .

Keep your thinking and conversations moving. Use this organizer as a work-in-progress. Iterate through the questions. As long as you have talented people to manage, you will have occasions to use it.

a summary

In the introduction to this book we posed some puzzles about managing talented people. We also encouraged you to pick your own way through our answers, a route that served your particular needs. As we approach the back cover, this seems like a good place to offer a summary of what we've been saying.

Let's review our puzzles in reverse order.

What exactly do people mean by talent?

What we have been arguing is that people are not clear about what they mean by talent. It's an alluring word, but it incorporates a bundle of differing expectations. Managers expect superior performance and creativity. Talent expects opportunity, development, independence. We need to disentangle and recognize these different expectations in order to manage them.

Why are the most talented often the most rewarding people to have in your team, but the most challenging to manage?

This is because talented people tend to be superior performers and at the same time complex and urgent in their motivations. They can give a lot, but they expect a lot too. And promptly. Talented people are among the managerial challenges that don't wait to be picked up.

They come at you.

They demand your attention.

If organizations are so aware of the need to retain talent, why don't they seem to be getting any better at it?

Because, when it comes to managing talented people, the action is at the level of individual managers and their individual talents. This is where the talent wars will be lost or won. In the quality of these individual interactions. Yes, it's important for organizations to be attractive places to work, to be employers of choice. Yes, it's important for organizations to review their talent pools, to assess potential, make development plans and provide programmes. But the action of managing talented people is more immediate than all that; it takes place in the moment, as manager and talent succeed, or fail, to meet each other's expectations.

Consequently, organizations will only get better at retaining their talent if their individual managers are up to the challenge. So this book has been written for those of you who are in the front trenches, managers of talented people. We set out to provide what we believe you need for this purpose:

◆ a deeper understanding of what is expected of and by talent;

◆ a few clear principles about your own role;

- a set of perspectives and moves to use as you handle your interactions;

- a structured means of connecting all of this to your own experience and situation.

This is our offering.

By our own logic, however, the most pressing puzzles of managing talented people are not ours but yours. The most important challenges are not ones that we can describe but the ones that you must resolve. What you finally take from this book, its conclusion, is one that you can only create for yourself.

the prequel (for those who want it)

What's going on out there?

We have put this bit in an appendix because it's not news. Unless you have been a contestant on one of those 'reality dramas' – marooned on a remote island or locked in an isolated house – you must have heard all about why the war for talent is a key battle of our time.

So why repeat it here? To emphasize that it needs action on your part. We want you to accept one thing – the world has changed. You must not get stuck in the trap of discussing whether people are important or whether today's new workers really want different things. Noah did not stand around with Mrs Noah and debate exactly how high the floods were or that perhaps God might just have a change of heart. He saw what was going on and acted accordingly. So must you.

This book is about how to manage talented people, not whether to. Therefore this 'why' bit is brief. We have included it because we make some assertions about the nature of talent, particularly in the first section, that have as their basis the global shifts that are going on. We want you to accept our perspective and focus on its application. Having a shared view of the broader environmental trends will help that.

So, if you've done this 'big picture' stuff to death already – glance at the section headings over the next few pages, and if they are all too painfully familiar, then proceed without delay back to the book (pass GO, even if you do not collect £200).

If you are now feeling uneasy that by some strange quirk of fate the whole talent revolution has passed you by, rest easy. The next few pages will provide a brief summary of what everyone else has been saying. Thereby justifying having saved yourself the trouble of reading it all before.

Before we begin

A couple of quick caveats before we get into the meat.

Looking at big trends is a funny business. It is partly retrospective (what data do we have about what has been happening?) and partly predictive (what therefore will the future be?). Doing it well is a fine art. We are not expert futurologists. Our concern here is to highlight how things are now. To ask you to pay attention to some broad trends that have made the present different from the past.

Our purpose is to help you avoid the much fabled 'boiled frog syndrome'. You know the one – a frog placed into cold water will stay in that water as its temperature is increased, to the point where it will boil alive. The same frog (presumably before being boiled) will leap out of hot water if dropped straight in. We are less sensitive to incremental changes, to the point where we don't notice. Accept the direction of our analysis and avoid being boiled alive.

Newton said that for every action there was an equal and opposite reaction. For every trend it seems there is always a counter trend, though not necessarily balanced. We have focused on the major forces, but beware – in the world of people, generalizations seldom apply. Throughout this book we encourage you to be adept at understanding your situation, to spot the specific clues. Take these trends as pointers, don't become their slaves.

Enough already. To the trends . . .

The technological shift

Really no excuse for missing this one – technology, particularly information technology, has dramatically changed our society. Here we want to draw your attention to a number of the key impacts on our working lives.

The simplest has to do with speed – the pace of change. At the heart of this is Moore's law – after Gordon Moore, the then chairman of Intel – the observation that every 18 months it is possible to double the number of transistor circuits etched on a computer chip. Doesn't sound too exciting, but the consequences are, as Boston Consulting Group's Philip Evans and Thomas Wurster point out in their book *Blown to Bits* (Harvard Business School Press, 2000). It implies a 10-fold increase in memory and processing power every five years, 100-fold every 10 years and 1000-fold every 15. The law has worked for the past 50 years and is predicted to last the next 50. We have become change junkies – hooked on the next great gizmo.

At the heart of this is Moore's law – after Gordon Moore, the then chairman of Intel – the observation that every 18 months it is possible to double the number of transistor circuits etched on a computer chip.

Not only does this mean things literally happen faster, but corresponding innovation means they also happen differently. You don't have to be very old to remember life without mobile phones or e-mail. This innovation has given us a second key shift, a move to connectivity. Actually the key thing is connectivity combined with the ability to have sitting in the spare room, or on the dining table, the basic means to do your job. People today are not suddenly looking for new ways of working on a whim – they are doing so because they can. The 'means of production' are now cheap and 'housable'.

Technology has influenced not only the pace of work and the location, but the very nature of it as well. A whole new profession – IT – has emerged and many of the traditional ones have changed too. Information, or more accurately knowledge, is power. In this world an individual can have a very dramatic impact – one person can make the difference. The high performer in the organization is no longer 10% more productive, but creates 10 times the impact.

Many of the new skills, of the new age, are portable. They translate across industries. So not only can people choose to supply their skills in a new way, the demand for them is more flexible too.

So the technological shift is producing a more urgent worker, one who knows that being good is very valuable and one who has choice in the way he or she delivers his or her skills. But there are other forces at play, building on the impact of technology.

The economic shift

So today's worker more often has the means to switch companies, but what about a motive? That too, since the downsizing exploits of many companies over the past decade. The traditional contract of lifetime employment in exchange for loyalty and commitment has, for many, been broken. Employers have been forced to reduce costs as the pressures of competition have increased. The same technology that has freed workers has also freed competitors. Now competing on a global scale is possible and, with ever increasing cost pressure, often necessary.

Running businesses on a global basis has brought with it other important trends. For example, the much lamented move of labour-intensive industries, such as manufacturing, to low-cost economies.

This has fuelled the economic growth of the developing nations and forced the focus of the developed onto the high-value, knowledge-rich activities. It is not only our individual businesses that depend on the knowledge worker, it is increasingly whole national economies. The consequential demand for the good knowledge workers is further threatened by the developing world. These are now large economies, which need managing and need to be supported in their own advances. Where is this coming from? The same place, of course, from the talent pool in the developed countries.

Talent – critical **and** scarce. Sounds expensive.

Sounds like doom and gloom for the developed world. But no. The transition to the so-called 'service sector economy' has brought unprecedented individual prosperity. The overall standard of living has been raised, but specifically the talent in organizations has what might be termed an 'expectation of comfort'. Most employees today have never suffered true hardship. The purpose of having work is not to survive, but something else. At the same time this has underlined that for many 'money' does not equal 'happiness'.

Available cash is not only a phenomenon affecting the individual. Capital has been, and is, more freely available then ever before. The 'dotcom' boom probably illustrated the excesses of this – new ventures seemingly getting financial support based on very little foundation. But looking over a longer period of time there has been a steady increase in venture capital available and consequently in the number of business start-ups.

The economic forces compound the technological. Both providing means and motive for a different approach to work, from both employer and employee. Before drawing the strands of this together, a third and final angle on these trends.

The social shift

One of the themes emerging from this discussion is the increased choice available for the individual, especially the talented. A power derived from choice, enabled by technology, financed by the economy. This freedom of choice is reflected in the diversity of patterns our lives now lead. Traditional institutions, which put boundaries around what was possible, have diminished – families, marriage, religion to name but three. The role of women has changed dramatically. Arguably while often increasing the complexity of our lives it has also increased our mobility as workers, if only because we seem to be willing to suffer the inconvenience for the sake of progress.

The world of work also takes on a new mantle, one of being an important source of purpose. The reducing influence of the traditional institutions risks leaving a void. Why are we here? Having reached a level of prosperity, we have moved way beyond just survival. As Maslow put it, we have moved up the hierarchy of needs to the top – self-actualization. We are increasingly intolerant of work that we find meaningless.

Not only do we seek meaning from our work, but also our life outside work. It is no longer enough just to work, we have to have a life as well and it needs to be in balance. Work–life balance is one of the new buzzwords of our time. It risks being a misleading one, as many buzzwords are. Work and life are not two separate things, so how can they be in balance?

The worker of today

Trends in technology, economics and in society itself have changed the way many people view work and their relationship to it. These changes are not temporary, they are grounded in structural change in our lives.

The knowledge worker of today is:

◆ well-off;

◆ more mobile;

◆ individual, less deferential;

◆ faced with, and empowered by, more choice;

- searching for meaning in their lives;
- seeking self-respect and personal growth;
- and doing it all at speed.

These people are different and the need for them has become more acute. Like it or not, organizations find themselves in the talent wars. The battlegrounds may be between organizations, but the outcome will be determined within organizations, by the individual managers responsible for managing talented people.

index